1968

TODAY'S AUTHORS EXPLORE A YEAR OF

REBELLION, REVOLUTION, AND CHANGE

EDITED BY **MARC ARONSON**

AND **SUSAN CAMPBELL BARTOLETTI**

CANDLEWICK PRESS

For James Cross Giblin and Russell Freedman,
kind and generous researchers, writers, and friends
who have lit the way for so many of us

INTRODUCTION

Nineteen sixty-eight was a year of seismic shifts and splits. In this collection of nonfiction stories, you'll read about this pivotal year, when generations clashed and the world seemed to wobble, trembling on the edge of some vast change — violent confrontation, assassinations, people power, scientific discovery, and triumph.

Story after story records a split: a generation gap that arose between disaffected youth and their elders, high-school and college students who clashed with the values of their parents, a rebellious spirit that drove young people to challenge mainstream politicians and the establishment, activists who clashed with repressive leaders, and repressive leaders who wielded power through force. But the stories also depict negative views of those same sixty-eighters in the eyes of workers and the poor — people for whom the activists claimed to be speaking. Is that perhaps a lesson from 1968 too often missed?

Some of the authors recall their experiences living in 1968; some have researched the events of the year. Paul Fleischman recalls his desire to strike out on his own and take a bicycle ride; Kate MacMillan recounts a revolution she joined in Paris. Laban Carrick Hill records growing up on the wrong side of a history that Kekla Magoon explores from precisely the opposite perspective. Kekla writes about an intense moment in Robert Kennedy's life that Mark Kurlansky experienced firsthand.

We followed our interests: Jim Murphy, an accomplished runner, gives us the drama of the 200-meter-dash ceremony at the Mexico Olympics, while Omar Figueras tells us about the bloody clashes between young people and government forces in Mexico City that preceded the Olympic Games. Jennifer Anthony considers the many roles of racism in the Columbia University protests.

Lenore Look, who speaks Chinese and is interested in investigating her heritage, explores the Red Guard's role in China's Cultural Revolution and the silence around it; David Lubar, who found his calling as a comic writer, surveys the comedians who transformed humor into a political weapon. Susan Campbell Bartoletti tunes into the counterculture Yippies and their invasion of the Chicago Democratic National Convention, while Mark Kurlansky describes another kind of invasion: Russian tanks that rolled into Prague.

Loree Griffin Burns, an accomplished biologist, looks at the code-breaking race behind the year's Nobel Prize in her subject. Marc Aronson uses his personal experiences to look back and then his historian's skill to find a key — and not well-known — piece of the 1968 story.

Elizabeth Partridge's prose poem weaves through the book, letting us feel the personal and emotional impact of the nightly news — a kind of verbal forecast of the crawlers we see on our TV sets today.

Nineteen sixty-eight was a sobering year. Losing Dr. King and Bobby Kennedy was an ending, not a beginning. The riots, the assassinations, the uprisings of young people gave us Richard Nixon. As a so-called law-and-order candidate, Nixon won the presidential race by playing simultaneously to the lingering segregationist sentiments of the white South and the seemingly more racially liberal but still uneasy northern suburbs and by promising that he had a "secret plan" to get the United States out of the war in Vietnam. Many view the 2016 presidential election as a redux of the 1968 election, brought about by a similar coalition of white Americans who felt threatened by a more multicultural America and left behind by a globalizing economy.

Today seismic political activity is once again sending vibrations around the globe. The generations are spinning, with outsiders and new parties winning in one country after another and causes such as caring for the planet animating waves of protest. Are we in for a new 1968?

Stories matter. True stories matter. Nonfiction writers write for story in the same way that fiction writers do. We share a love of idea and words, a love for art and craft.

One of the joys of creating this nonfiction anthology was the opportunity to showcase different ways of framing and writing nonfiction. In this collection, you'll find authors who relied on memory, who conducted interviews, and who utilized archival material and scholarship. Some focused tightly on one incident or subject; others offered a broad exposition of a movement.

Each approach yields different voices, different stories, different styles of writing, different points of view. There is no reason—indeed, no excuse—for nonfiction to be bland, voiceless, and uniform.

This is where one of us—Marc—interjects, saying, "There are two common misunderstandings about nonfiction: (1) that nonfiction equals facts and (2) that since experts keep changing their views, and since even in everyday life, we all have differing points of view, 'it is all relative.' Facts are useful in nonfiction, but the heart of nonfiction is thinking: making a contention, a case, a story. A fact may be important, but it is not an explanation; while each of us, even an expert, may have a different approach to history, those views are not equally true. Interpretations can be compared, contrasted, evaluated. We will never have perfect knowledge, but we can determine which of our current views is more likely. Indeed, that is what we must do: compare, contrast, judge."

And this is where the other one of us—Susan—interrupts Marc, agreeing with him but questioning the word *relative,* asking, "If what we know—knowledge—changes over time, is it contingent upon time and place and therefore relative? Is it possible to then understand the past and make meaning about the past in different, even contradictory ways, based on new facts and new knowledge? Is it possible to have multiple ownerships of the past? Is this the reason that so many interpretations of the past can be told from different points of view?"

This is where we agree: Nonfiction is a commitment to a research and writing process. Nonfiction writers utilize the same literary devices that fiction writers do, but we do not invent characters, dialogue, or other details of fact. We share our sources, research, and reasoning behind the writing. We're open to challenge. If we come across facts or interpretations that upend what we initially believed, we examine, reconsider, and rewrite accordingly. We must be willing to be wrong. In this way, we are faithful to the process of exploration and discovery—and to a reasoned construction of our subject.

Each story in this book could be written again, framed from another point of view. Another edition of the book you are reading could be written from the point of view of those who detested the student revolts at Columbia University and in Paris, or from the point of view of Chicago mayor Richard Daley and the Chicago police force or a National Guardsman, or from a perspective that shows 1968 as a key point in the growth of political conservatism, evangelical movements, and resistance to a woman's access to birth control and abortion.

No matter your point of view, we hope our book allows you to visit an earlier time when global tectonic plates seemed to be inexorably smashing into one another, even as you make sense of the quakes taking place around us now. What political forces are gathering now that will shape the next fifty years—and what role do you want to play in them?

What will be your revolution?

1968

January
February
March

NIGHTLY NEWS
Elizabeth Partridge

═══ WINTER ═══

Every night it's the same: the Vietnam War invades our living rooms. Six o'clock news, eleven o'clock news. Steel-helmeted GIs tread single file through stifling jungles, slog through rice fields. President Johnson calls it the *steaming soil* of Vietnam. Machine guns spit bullets, and men belly-crawl, shoot, kill, and die.

Safe at home, I watch a GI flick his Zippo lighter, ignite a thatched roof. With a roar the hut explodes into flames, then another hut, and soon the whole village is a raging inferno of fire and smoke. Women and children stand mute, eyes wide with terror. Young men are blindfolded, arms bound tight behind their backs, taken away for interrogation.

In flat voices, newscasters tell us how many Americans died today on the steaming soil of Vietnam, defending democracy from Communism. There is a daily count of enemy dead, as well as villagers, regretfully caught in cross fire.

I'm with the marchers who fill American streets, chanting, protesting, carrying signs. Up early on Saturday, bus to San Francisco, walking, chanting. *Peace now, peace now.*

And then one day, the news isn't the same.

January 30. Communist North Vietnamese launch the Tet Offensive, pouring down into South Vietnam.

JANUARY 1968
American combat deaths: 1,202
South Vietnamese ally combat deaths: 2,905
Vietnamese enemy combat deaths: 15,217
Vietnamese civilian deaths: 618

Fighting in Vietnam is city by city, street by street. Rat-a-tat-tat of firefights ricochet off my walls. North Vietnamese troops and Viet Cong take on South Vietnamese and American troops. Civilians grab children, run, run, run. The American Embassy in Saigon—a gleaming new building, symbol of our power—is attacked by the Viet Cong.

The whistles of incoming mortar rounds scream in through my television. U.S. fighter planes roar across Vietnam's skies to drop burning napalm, phosphorus, and cluster bombs.

I cut PE class, stay out through English and algebra, joining the marchers who fill the streets protesting, chanting. *Hell, no, we won't go.*

Man walking beside me says Vietnamese body counts are lies. Villagers get killed, called the enemy.

My stomach twists tight in a knot, doesn't let go. Can this be true?

FEBRUARY 1968
American combat deaths: 2,124
South Vietnamese ally combat deaths: 5,025
Vietnamese enemy combat deaths: 17,371
Vietnamese civilian deaths: 543

President Johnson says we beat back the Communists, calls it a military victory. Now we need to win the war.

Martin Luther King Jr. wrestled with his conscience, decided he couldn't stay silent on Vietnam. Keeps speaking out. Look who's fighting this war, he says. Black men. Brown men. Poor white men. Look who we're dropping napalm on. Grandmothers. Children. Babies.

Those nightly news death numbers keep coming, like a church bell tolling during a medieval plague.

It's ringing for teens like me. Girls watching boyfriends, brothers, and friends head off to war. Boys old enough to fight, too young to vote. Getting drafted into the army, even if they don't want to go. Hearts tight with fear, words of bravado and patriotism tumbling out of their mouths.

It's ringing for Vietnamese mothers and fathers and children, soldiers on both sides.

Marching, chanting. *Hey, hey, LBJ, how many kids did you kill today?*

Protesters throw rocks, break windows. Cops in riot gear swing billy clubs and throw tear gas canisters, chase people down. Marchers flash peace signs as they're dragged away. It feels different, frightening. I stay on the edges, ready to run.

March 16. Bobby Kennedy tells us he's after Johnson's job, says he's running for president. He's going for the Democratic nomination. The war is tearing our country in half, Kennedy says. He wants to end the bloodshed in Vietnam, close the gaps between rich and poor, black and white. Calls our policies disastrous and divisive.

He'd get my vote, if I could. Bobby Kennedy and Martin Luther King Jr. hold our hope for change.

MARCH 1968
American combat deaths: 1,543
South Vietnamese ally combat deaths: 2,570
Vietnamese enemy combat deaths: 24,086
Vietnamese civilian deaths: 287

BIKER'S ED

I stood over my Schwinn ten-speed. My friend Jeff was at the ready on his Raleigh. We were simultaneously giddy and jittery. It was a Saturday morning, with Monday a school holiday. Our parents had agreed to let us miss Tuesday and Wednesday. We might have been the heroes on page one of a fairy tale. Or the fools. We were about to set off into the wide world.

Where were we headed? North.

Why? Because we were sixteen. And because it was 1968.

We careened down Santa Monica's Seventh Street hill, gravity delivering us to Pacific Coast Highway. The light turned green and we made a right, heading up the coast away from Los Angeles. We had no inkling of the future trips that, like chess games, would all begin with this move.

I'd tied a sleeping bag to my rear rack. The metal baskets on either side were half empty. A tent in case it rained? No need. Sixteen-year-olds are mad optimists. Water? A single metal canteen. Navigation? A paper map of California. An iPod and earbuds? Are you crazy? Those were thirty years away. Music for us was shelved in the brain. Entertainment on the road meant singing to yourself.

We passed Sunset Boulevard, then Malibu Pier at mile ten. I'd scouted Malibu's canyons in the past, but the ever-present need to head back had kept me from riding beyond the pier. Not this time. The trip was truly on.

Leaving home can be essential to survival. Maple seeds' wings let them escape their parents' shade. My parents were maples and had made no objections to the trip. My father, after all, hadn't been drawn to his parents' clothing store and had spent his entire sixteenth summer traveling California, performing magic for a living. Though I got on well with my parents, and beachside Santa Monica was hard to top as a place to grow up, I didn't need any prodding to leave the nest. I'd begun plotting my escape back in seventh grade.

That's when I started pouring myself a bowl of cereal at night and opening the *Los Angeles Times* to the weather page. Weather barely existed in Santa Monica. I'd never felt air colder than 45 degrees. Which was why my eye was drawn to the list of Canadian cities. Check out Halifax, Nova Scotia: High: 4. Low: -22. The very look of those numbers made me hungry to be there. Bangor, Maine: snow. Boston: freezing rain. Those luckies! Some hormone was urging me to plant myself among them, as far from home as possible.

My family home was large. We had two cars in the garage. The year before, the hit movie *The Graduate* had asked whether a house in the suburbs and a self-defrosting fridge were likely to bring us happiness. It answered with a resounding no. When the main character is offered a hot tip on a successful career—"Plastics!"—the theater audience around me howled. But if money wasn't the key to fulfillment, what was?

The books, music, and movies around me didn't give a definitive answer. The key was to be searching. Instead of marching straight from school into some soul-ravaging job, the idea was to stop and think, to know yourself and the world and to decide what was truly important before going forward.

Great, but how?

Some used drugs, seeking insights and new experiences in the maze of the mind.

Some used books to expand their boundaries and find new models. The two most commonly seen books in my high school's halls that year were *Soul on Ice* by Eldridge Cleaver and Hermann Hesse's novel *Siddhartha*. These weren't assigned reading but part of the quest, the first book detailing an African-American man's political development, the second a search for truth in the time of Buddha.

But the quest could take another form: travel. This too opened one to strange places and new people. The purpose was less to get somewhere than to learn things along the way. Jack Kerouac's *On the Road* was the book that launched a million such trips, a word-jazz account of pinballing around the country with no goal other than experience.

You need money to travel, right? Wrong. Did Buddha reach for his Visa card? He walked and held out his begging bowl. Sixties travelers did something similar. Instead of a bowl, they held out their thumbs. Hitchhiking was the preferred means of travel not only because it was free but because it was a teacher, a surrender to chance that put you in touch with the mysterious workings of the universe. It was also an expression of trust and community that brought you into contact with like-minded folks. The person who picked you up might become a lasting friend. Might offer you a place to sleep. Might pass along an STD. All part of the journey.

Jeff and I were a little young to hitch, but biking had many of the same advantages. It was almost free; all you had to do was refuel every few hours with a package of those little white sugar doughnuts. Though it was more reliable than hitching, it still brought the unexpected. Something else important: it took you out into nature.

Mainstream culture was all about cities; the countryside was an afterthought. Our generation turned that around. Communes sprang up in the middle of nowhere. The ancient arts of growing food and building shelter were relearned. Hiking and backpacking took off, spurred further by Colin Fletcher's 1968 book, *The Complete Walker*. The suburbs only taught you how to rake leaves, but if you'd had the good fortune to grow up shoveling manure and milking cows, you were somebody. Teat cred.

Which explains why we were pedaling north. We lived on the edge of LA. To the south and east lay freeways, concrete, smog. To the north: redwoods, fog, empty beaches. The only American city that had any lure for us was San Francisco, the capital of hippie culture. Or better, Vancouver, given that Canada had stayed out of Vietnam, was mainly wilderness, and had William Shatner, Joni Mitchell, and *Never Cry Wolf* author Farley Mowat on its team. Do the math. Clearly cooler than us.

Jeff sported the Canadian maple leaf among the regalia on his military jacket, which could have come from the cover of the Beatles' *Sgt. Pepper's Lonely Hearts Club Band*. He wore John Lennonesque wire-rims and would have been the band's sole redhead. I was more Ringo, smaller and less conspicuous, a comfort the first time the trip made good on its promise to introduce us to people we hadn't known we'd meet. We were in the town of Oxnard, where we'd stopped that first afternoon to get a drink at a restaurant. As we walked in, the Hells Angels were walking out.

Black leather vests, beards, and brawn, belonging to the most notorious motorcycle gang in the land. They were trust and freedom's flip side, the side that could make the road a scary place. I'd assured my parents we'd be safe with the words "It's not like we'll run into the Hells Angels." We stepped aside to let them pass.

"Nice jacket," one of them muttered to Jeff. We were speechless. Maybe, I thought, he'd remember us and keep the others from hacking us to death on a beach. When they started up their motorcycles, the restaurant's entire population—who'd probably gone stiff from pretending not to look at them—rushed to the windows to watch them go. I hoped they'd head south. They turned to the north.

After our drinks, we followed. We passed the first cypress tree, an emblem of the fabled North. Right on! By that time it was late afternoon. Where would we sleep? We hadn't thought that far. Planning was for travel agents. We'd envisioned a round-trip to my sister's at the University of California Santa Barbara, a hundred miles north of Santa Monica. Beyond that, the details were up for grabs.

The sun was sinking and so was our energy by the time we hit Carpenteria. I looked down at the odometer attached to my front wheel. We'd ridden seventy-five miles. We were wildly impressed. Lacking Facebook, we shared this news via the cutting-edge communications technology of the day: by feeding dimes into a pay phone and calling our friends.

Dinner was French bread smeared with cream cheese, eaten on the beach. Food had never tasted so good. As the only nearby campground was full, we paid eight dollars for a dingy motel room that featured a fist-shaped hole in the wall. Wow. Real reality. Or at least a different corner of it from the one we'd have seen if we'd been traveling with our parents. We'd brought a copy of *Alfred Hitchcock's Mystery Magazine* to read aloud in the evenings. At roughly the same time, Jeff fell asleep listening and I fell asleep reading.

We cruised through Santa Barbara the next day, zipped around UCSB, and found my sister's apartment. Unfortunately there wasn't room for us to stay. No problem. Travel was dancing with chance, right? When we returned to our bikes, Jeff's sleeping bag was gone.

Whoa. That wasn't chance—that was theft! So much for trust and community. We borrowed my sister's sleeping bag and spent hours

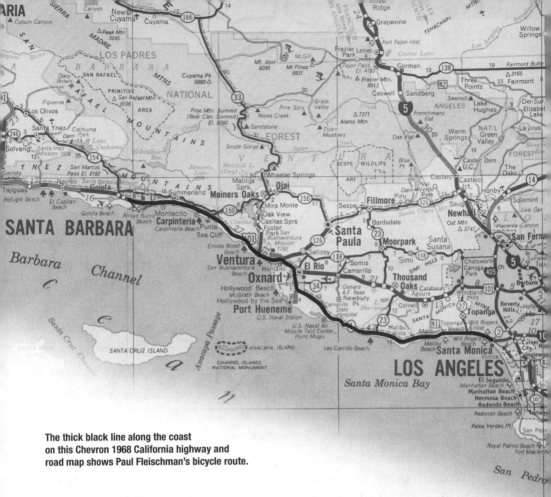

The thick black line along the coast
on this Chevron 1968 California highway and
road map shows Paul Fleischman's bicycle route.

after dark searching for a safe place to sleep, finally choosing an unlit patch of grass near a road.

In the middle of the night came the moment I'd feared. I opened my eyes to see two big men walking toward us. Jeff was sleeping deeply. My mouth went dry, and I waited to experience my first fractured skull and/or armed robbery. Then they stopped, aimed a flashlight at us, and, miraculously, turned around. I realized they were driving off in a police car. They'd probably been checking to make sure we were alive. I understood why in the morning, when I found we'd been sleeping on a traffic island.

We retraced our way down the coast, making discoveries. Bananas don't really roast like marshmallows. Sleeping on sand is like sleeping on concrete. It's a bad idea to get separated from your trip partner if the cell phone hasn't yet been invented. We sweated up all those Malibu hills we'd screamed down, then suddenly we were home, my odometer reading 245. And then the trip's ripples spread.

We and our friends realized that you could cover some serious ground on a bicycle. "You are now free to move about the country" was our motto before it belonged to Southwest Airlines. That summer, a bunch of our friends rode our route and pronounced bike-camping cool. In the summer of 1970, four of them got a ride with their bikes up to Vancouver and proceeded to pedal, take the train, and hitchhike the entire breadth of Canada. Two years after that, I did the opposite, riding up the coast to Vancouver, taking a train across Canada, then riding another one thousand miles in the East.

That second trip epitomized the quest. I had no idea of my destination. A chance meeting with a couple in an Oregon campground planted the seed of a lifelong friendship and pointed me to their corner of New Hampshire. Instead of returning to college in California, I stayed, gorging on new experiences for two years. I hitched around New England, lived out in the country, split wood with an ax, learned the names of the birds and flowers and constellations. The house I lived in had been built in 1770, its first occupants' tombstones right there on the property. I was sleeping in the same bedroom many of them had slept in. A shiver of identification went through me, and one day I knew what I wanted to study when I went back to college: history. That and natural history would end up informing many of the books I'd later write.

In 1969, the Hells Angels were hired as security for a Rolling Stones concert in Altamont in the California hills, where one of them stabbed an armed concertgoer to death. Some people date the death of '60s culture to that event. I date it to that stolen sleeping bag. Assaults and murders caused hitchhiking to fade out as a common mode of transport in the 1970s. A new generation of moneymakers filled business schools in the 1980s. Today's young people are flocking to the downtowns of cities. Pendulums swing.

And then they swing again. The urge to explore the world and the self never died out. Nature and justice still inspire. Generosity and community are the fuel for today's crowd-funding campaigns. If farmers' markets are any gauge, a new generation is delighting in tilling the soil. These days the acceptance of gap years acknowledges the importance of the quest.

Maybe you'll take one.

Maybe travel with a friend.

Possibly bicycles will be involved.

Have a great trip!

THE RED GUARD

LENORE LOOK

Mention "1968" and "China" to a Chinese person, and the reaction is often the same: a quick, almost imperceptible inhale, as though just before being pushed underwater.

"Why do you want to ask about that?" my mother snapped when I raised the topic, hoping she'd point me to a friend or relative who lived in China at the time. "People aren't going to talk to you." Asking about the Cultural Revolution is tantamount to asking for state secrets, and I was putting myself and others in danger, she insisted. "Don't do it. Give the story back."

My mother has always been fearful and pulls herself in like a turtle at the slightest whiff of anything wild, real or imagined. But I, still quick to rebel against what I see as her old Chinese ways, will rush toward the first scent of danger, like a crazy squirrel after a nut, and fling myself headfirst off the cliff.

The year 1968 marked the height of the Cultural Revolution in China, when the violent, student-propelled political movement exploded on an unprecedented scale and reverberated around the world. Student activists calling themselves Chairman Mao's Red Guards, or *hong weibing* ("red-scarf soldiers"), had run amok since 1966, smashing, looting, burning, and murdering—at the urging of their country's leader, Mao Zedong, who had shut down schools nationwide so that students could take to the streets. As a party circular from May 1966 put it, "Chairman Mao often says that there is no construction without destruction. . . . Put destruction first, and in the process you have construction. . . . Thoroughly criticize and repudiate the reactionary bourgeois ideas in the sphere of academic work, education, journalism, literature and art, and publishing, and seize the leadership in these cultural spheres."

No school? Go wild? Who wouldn't love a leader like that?

In reality this was a calculated move by the elder statesman to remove his political enemies. By calling on the youth to violently denounce all authority, and giving them license to remove their teachers and principals, Mao knew that he could later turn them against powerful officials. A strong, modern China, he added, needed to be rid of the "four olds": old ideas, old customs, old habits, and old culture. What teenager doesn't hate old?

Mobs of angry Red Guards responded by torturing and killing their teachers and school officials in public "struggle sessions," ransacking their homes, burning books, destroying libraries full of historical texts, desecrating temples and cemeteries, destroying churches and mosques, smashing cultural relics, beating anyone appearing to have middle-class tendencies (such as wearing western shoes or clothing), and attacking one another. China descended into chaos as Mao prohibited the police from interfering with Red Guard activities, and anyone doing so faced consequences as a counterrevolutionary.

By 1968, foreign embassies burned; foreign companies fled; Chinese workers joined the revolution, leading to a widespread food shortage and strict rationing of food and goods. The bloodshed escalated into virtual civil war in July, when Mao finally sent the army to put an end to the Red Guards' reign of terror. By the year's end, up to sixteen million people labeled as intellectuals—which meant any educated young people, middle-schoolers and older—were ordered to leave the cities and go into the countryside to work among the peasants.

By some accounts, the Red Guards inspired the student mobilization in Paris and its violent clashes with the police in May 1968. Mavis Gallant, who covered the Paris riots for the *New Yorker,* wrote: "The occupied Sorbonne . . . in the vast forecourt, a table piled with Mao's red book, selling at one franc twenty." And she recalled a friend saying, "It is the ugliness that attracts them."

By the time the Cultural Revolution ended with the death of Mao in 1976, up to two hundred million people suffered from chronic malnutrition because of the crippled economy; about twenty million people, including the student activists, had been displaced to rural areas to be "reeducated" by peasants; and up to one and a half million citizens had been executed or driven to suicide.

The more I thought about the scale of terror and damage that they achieved, the more I was certain that the Red Guards were at the center of whatever needed to be said about 1968 China. What made them do it? What did they achieve? How did engaging in the atrocities change or shape their lives? What effect, if any, does it have on China today? What is there to be discovered that would stir us to think deeply, intelligently, and even courageously, about a country in dark times? Not just China, but all countries. Do we view our own dark legacies differently? In the United States, are we encouraging independent thinking about violence and white privilege? Have we collected the wider reflections of the members of the KKK on their history of lynching and terror, and their violent legacy that continues into the present day? And what is it about our own unchecked gun violence and mass shootings in our communities and schools that we cannot confront and resolve? How does 1968 China speak to the United States today? I had no idea. But I set about to interview former Red Guards to get the story directly from them.

Eagerly I e-mailed my best contact in China, a smart young woman who works in children's publishing, who, by the mission of her work, would certainly be on board to help me find the teenagers of yesterday to speak to the teenagers of today. Her answer came swiftly:

It's a surprise to know Candlewick Press plan to let kids know something about 1968. In my parents' opinion, their child-hood is full of innocent and interesting memories. They took part in this historical situation in their way. Crazy but still be a great fortune to them.

However, no people I know is a Red Guard. . . . They will glorify horrible things. . . .

That's the reason I am not sure whether to ask my elders to tell their stories to you.

Our e-mails ping-ponged back and forth but went nowhere. Sadly, I realized too late that I had underestimated the complexities the Chinese face in discussing those years, especially with a foreigner. And my direct, American approach of asking explicitly for something I wanted — to talk to former *hong weibing* — sabotaged my best hope for interviewing them in China.

"You can't use the words 'Red Guards' or '*hong weibing,*'" my friend Nancy Kremers said with a gasp over the phone when I told her what had happened. I should have called her first. Nancy had served as general counsel in the U.S. Embassy in Beijing during the Obama administration and knew how to navigate the precipitous mountains of asking for things in a roundabout way. "You must say 'sent-down youth,'" she said. "They'll talk to you as 'sent-down youth' because even President Xi says his years spent in the countryside were a positive influence on his life."

The current president, Xi Jinping, who was thirteen when the pandemonium erupted, has rarely spoken in public about his experiences from 1966 to 1968, and his close contemporaries have refused to speak to foreign journalists about those years. The Chinese government condemned the movement in a resolution in 1981, stating, "History has shown that the 'cultural revolution' initiated by a leader labouring under a misapprehension and capitalized on by counter-revolutionary cliques, led to domestic turmoil and brought catastrophe to the Party, the state and the whole people."

Before and after the condemnation, the government and official news outlets maintained a strict silence on the decade. Then, in 2016, as the fiftieth anniversary approached, an editorial appeared in the *Global Times,* a party tabloid, warning against Internet discussions and any talk that might lead to a "cleavage in people's ideological understanding" of the period. It reminded readers that since a 1981 resolution "made the authoritative conclusion of the utter denial of the Cultural Revolution," discussions should not depart from the party's decided politics or thinking.

Outside China, much has been written about the turmoil, but I couldn't find any extensive look at the radical students themselves. Aside from a handful of memoirs written by former Red Guards, there was no wider view of reflections from an entire generation that chose rebellion and revolution over policy and politics as a vehicle for social change. The more I searched, the less I found. How did a force of tens of millions just disappear? From four memoirs, I learned the following:

- The Red Guards are not to be mistaken for all the school-age children wearing red scarves. The ubiquitous red scarf was, and continues to be, a symbol of national pride, given out in schools as a reward for good behavior.

- The Red Guards were not about good behavior. They were about political and cultural cleansing.

- Not everyone was qualified to be a *hong weibing*.

- They were not the children of peasants; they were the sons and daughters of the elite.

- Membership was highly exclusive; students were handpicked by others who were certain they shared the right pedigree — their parents and grandparents were party officials, and they, in turn, saw themselves as the rightful heirs to power.

- The Red Guards were not a unified group but consisted of countless factions, each operating independently and in competition with others (like gangs in the United States).

- Anyone with the right family background, enough charisma, and a catchy name for a group, such as "Fearless Red Rebels" or "Great Wall Fighting Team," could start one.

- But Red Guards, too, found it challenging to show enough fervor to avoid becoming targets within their own cliques.

It was paltry information, tantamount to taking a microscope to a water buffalo.

Then my mother, still shaking her head in disapproval, jumped in to give CPR to my sputtering research. She called one of her relatives, Fan, who grew up in Guangzhou during the Cultural Revolution. Immediately, the woman volunteered her husband, who was a teenager then and was sent down from the North to live in the impoverished South.

When her husband declined to be interviewed, Fan offered to tell me her story. She was five when the violence began. She saw Red Guards beating people, and corpses in the streets. Her experiences were not dissimilar to what I had already read in memoirs and articles and seen in documentaries. She was a witness to the events but not a participant. She was not what I was looking for. Still, you can never tell where an interview will lead.

"I was in kindergarten when it started," she began. "But I didn't go to first grade until the revolution was over. They marched people through the streets with cones on their heads and signs around their necks. I watched from our second-floor window."

Fan's parents were not targets — they were factory workers — but she remembers *hong weibing* ransacking their neighbor's apartment and stealing everything. When bodies began hanging from trees in 1967, she and her younger brother were sent to live with relatives in their family's village, in the countryside away from the violence.

"How is your life still affected by what happened during that time?" I asked. What she said next was so obvious that it was unexpected, and delivered with such clarity that it was the sound of the earth rearranging her skirts to accommodate the truth.

"It stole my education," Fan said, looking at me squarely for the first time, as though she were a crossing guard facing down traffic. "I'm not an educated person today."

Silence.

We stared at each other, as into a mirror of the other life we might have lived. Her grandmother was my maternal great-grandfather's sister. We were born one ocean and one year apart. She saw brutalized corpses on her way to and from kindergarten. My walk to kindergarten was through a poor immigrant neighborhood in Seattle, not a war zone.

In this 1968 Chinese stamp, members of the Red Guard hold up Chairman Mao's Little Red Book, a collection of more than two hundred quotations, including this one: "Every Communist must grasp the truth, 'Political power grows out of the barrel of a gun.'"

During Fan's fifth-grade year, her class was sent to work on a vegetable farm, then in a flashlight factory, then in a car assembly plant. Around the same age, I went camping for the first time with my class and carried a flashlight—probably made in China. When she turned fifteen, she was sent again to work on a farm, where she carried human feces from the pit toilet to the fields as fertilizer, for two years. At fifteen, I carried my backpack to and from school. The only human excrement I saw was my own, and I flushed it away. With her farm-and-factory education, Fan went to work teaching elementary school, making thirty-two renminbi (about five U.S. dollars) a month, when I started high school. Around the time that she was assigned to a better-paying job in a factory, washing clothes for sixty-two renminbi (almost ten U.S. dollars) a month, I began my freshman year at Princeton.

I didn't know what to say. The Cultural Revolution had stacked her loss column and emptied her gains column. It wasn't the way things turned out in the memoirs written by former Red Guards. They all went back to school after serving their time in the countryside. Their lives improved beyond recognition as China transformed itself from a culture of ideology to one of economic reforms. Beginning in the late

1970s, the government reversed many of Mao's policies, opened China to the outside world, and, according to newspaper accounts, improved the lives of "many, but not most," Chinese. I had no idea that "many" referred to the privileged and "most" referred to everyone else.

I continued my search for a Red Guard (singular—I had scaled back my ambitions) in New York City's Chinatown. "Just ask for anyone willing to share stories about their lives as teenagers," advised Jeffrey Chen, the office manager at Greater Chinatown Community Association on Mosco Street, where free classes and social activities are offered to senior citizens. "Don't mention the Cultural Revolution, or any terms associated with it. Let them bring it up."

Five women came forward and generously shared their stories of joining the record exodus of millions of Chinese into Hong Kong during the height of the violence, their lives of extreme poverty, and their greatest loss—their educations.

"We were not allowed to attend school," said Lisa Szeto, fifty-nine. It was an experience common to all of them. Their parents feared that an education posed greater risks than benefits. But most said they simply needed to work for their families to survive. They labored in factories making wigs and/or took in piecework at home, needling sequins onto sweaters or stringing plastic flowers. If there was any money for tuition, their time in school was brief, but their brothers were allowed to stay longer. As refugees, their first homes were flimsy wooden structures that covered the steep hillsides of Hong Kong, like marooned rafts on a frozen sea. Disease and despair were uninvited guests in every family. Ill siblings died without medical treatment or were abandoned. Countless children filled the streets, roaming freely while parents toiled in the factories, many of which were set up outside.

This wasn't the story I was looking for, but it was the story that came looking for me: the hard lives of children during the Cultural Revolution. While the children of privilege made revolution in China, the children of peasants scrambled to survive. All the women I spoke with eventually immigrated to the United States and found their old lives of poverty in a new place. They spent their adult lives as seam-stresses, janitors, or kitchen help.

The memoirs of the Red Guards, on the other hand, revealed that their struggles consisted of getting into the right universities, obtain-ing admittance to the right academic departments, and manipulating authorities to land the right job assignments in the right locations. Often it took years, but in the end, they triumphed, and ultimately, most of the authors ended up in teaching positions in western univer-sities and publishing their stories of the indomitable human spirit over overwhelming odds.

Two stories. Rich and poor. Privilege and poverty. One story told candidly to a curious inquirer, the other silent, except for the care-fully curated events of memoirists. How does this duality affect China today?

We need only look around to see that another Chinese student rev-olution is under way. A record number of Chinese are studying abroad, nearly 330,000 in the United States alone in 2016.

And what of the children of rural peasants today?

Tens of millions of children (possibly more) who have moved with their parents from the countryside into cities for the lowest-wage jobs are banned from attending city schools. An estimated 300,000 million migrant workers (with an additional 13 million joining the ranks every year) often exceed the number of native residents in cities across China. But everyone must attend school where they were born. If you take the *gaokao*, the university entrance exam, you must also take it in your natal place. And if you were born in a city to migrant par-ents, you also lack urban registry (*hukou*) and are not allowed to go to school or take the *gaokao* anywhere but in your parents' *laojia* (origi-nal home). This has meant that children from remote provinces with limited resources — and often, underqualified teachers — don't stand a chance at getting into any top-tier universities, or even into a low-tier one. Your birthplace determines your life's path. Indeed, this system of privilege and poverty existed long before the revolution, as Mao noted in 1927: "In China education has always been the exclusive preserve of the landlords, and the peasants have had no access to it. . . . Ninety percent of the people have had no education."

My mom's education ended abruptly when, as a rural student, she failed to test into high school. This happened about a decade before the Cultural Revolution, during the Great Leap Forward. She had never said much about that period in her life; every accounting of her personal history seemed to begin in 1960, when she married my dad, an American, and immigrated to the United States. But as she watched me naively, stubbornly, and unsuccessfully search for a Red Guard, she revealed something of her past that surprised me.

"I went from village to village with my classmates doing skits about the virtues of Mao and the Communist Party," she said in her native Toisan dialect. "We needed to convince the farmers that it was good for them."

My mother, a daughter of peasants, a part of the propaganda machine? It was unbelievable. Did she know that people were starving? Or was she doing it *because* people were starving? Did she even have a choice? I had a million questions. But my mom, a forest of mysteries, closed up again after releasing the single bird.

Then I understood all at once that people who have lived through dark times are fearful of many things. Survival is paramount. Keeping quiet is vital. The lack of public reflection doesn't necessarily mean there hasn't been inward reflection and depthless remorse or shame. Chinese culture doesn't demand that everything understood be spoken. Regardless of education or economic level, every Chinese person carries around five thousand years of a collective identity. Five thousand years of dark times. Five thousand years of survival. Five thousand years of not demanding absolute truth when sizing up a single life or a vast empire. Five thousand years of preferring to remember people and events in a good light.

Red Guards will probably die with their stories because of their shame and fear of reprisal, a producer at a state-owned Shanghai TV station told me recently. People are starting to talk about the Cultural Revolution, he said. It's the 1989 Tiananmen Square uprising that is strictly verboten now. Ask anyone in their twenties about it, and no one has any idea or has only a vague notion of "something about a lot of people outside." The Chinese spark quickly and violently to injustices, he added. "They will fight [first]. No discussion." So the government restricts information to maintain stability.

I'm no closer to interviewing a Red Guard than when I began, but instead, I've found an unexpected prism through which to view my own country's reluctance to confront its history, and continuation, of sanctioned violence. The United States has less than three hundred years of history as a nation, no collective identity (which is not a bad thing), and our legacy of race-based violence began as soon as the first white newcomers met the first inhabitants. Our country has always created our own truths, institutionalized immoral behavior (including the eradication of Native Americans and the perpetuation of slavery, racism, and gun violence), and kept silent a system of advantages and disadvantages with so many gains in some columns that it has caused endemic blindness, and so many losses in others that the value of some lives has been reduced from three-fifths of a human being to the price of a clay pigeon for target practice. And as a society, we are not universally outraged.

The Chinese are silent because they are told to be. We are silent without being told. An all-American trait. What a strange thing to learn from 1968 China.

THE STUDENT VIEW FROM PARIS

Soixante-Huitards (Sixty-Eighters) from Hope to Rage

KATE MACMILLAN

Clash silken cymbals

Beat paper gongs

Kiss stone statues

Sing soundless songs

Walk on nails and air

Soixante-huit will never end

— Kate MacMillan, 1968 (revised 2017)

Nineteen sixty-eight . . . It was the year that changed lives. It was the year that average college students became radicalized into activists. It was the spring of hope and freedom and the summer of rage and sadness. It was the year that we took to the streets, and it was the year that we lost our innocence. It was the year that would bind us together as *soixante-huitards*, the activists of 1968.

Nineteen sixty-eight was the year of Vietnam antiwar marches, campus sit-ins and walkouts . . . France's month-long student revolution . . . Martin Luther King's assassination and the resulting riots . . . Bobby Kennedy's presidential campaign and assassination . . . It was the bloody riots at the Democratic National Convention and the Mexico

Olympics. It was a year that precipitated change and supported the status quo. It was a year that divided the nation and united student radicals. It was a time of hope and then a time of despair.

We were the first of the baby boomers. Unlike our parents, we did not experience the poverty of the Great Depression or the fear of World War II and the Korean War. We were the generation that would have superior educations, buy more consumer goods, live in suburban ranch houses with green lawns and *Leave It to Beaver* mothers. By 1968 this dream had lost its appeal for many of us. Feminism had taken hold; the Civil Rights Act of 1964, outlawing racial discrimination, was in place; the Equal Pay Act and birth control were a reality. America was finally waking up from the 1950s . . . and we *soixante-huitards* were the ones who would shake and shape this new world.

Can anyone accurately remember every event or speech from fifty years ago? Facts and words may be forgotten, but we remember the long discussions about peace, freedom, and equality. We were fueled by coffee, cigarettes, and camaraderie . . . always the camaraderie. We were the dreamers and true believers, angry and innocent and set upon making the world a better place. The French students' motto of *Égalité! Liberté! Sexualité!* belonged to all of us no matter our nationality. We were fomenting a cultural revolution that would radically change the stifling conservatism of our parents.

Nineteen sixty-eight . . . It was barely a year after the Summer of Love in San Francisco's Haight-Ashbury neighborhood and a year after the release of the Beatles' *Sgt. Pepper's Lonely Hearts Club Band*. It was two years after Huey Newton and Bobby Seale formed the Black Panther Party and less than two years after Muhammad Ali was convicted of draft evasion and stripped of his heavyweight title. It was five years after the Free Speech Movement at Berkeley, with the entrancing rhetoric of student leader Mario Savio. It was three years after the march to Selma and the Watts Riots. It was seven years after the murderous Freedom Riders summer. And then there was the never-ending Vietnam War and the draft. . . . These were the pivotal events that inspired our demands for peace, freedom, justice, and racial equality. These were events that led us to Paris in May 1968.

We *soixante-huitards* were the dreamers, steadfast and unshaken. We believed we could remake the world, we believed in free love, we believed in the lyrics of our music, we believed in free speech, we believed in our right to demonstrate, and we believed that we could end the Vietnam War. From the University of California at Berkeley to the Université Paris–Sorbonne, these beliefs formed the psyche of every 1968 student revolutionary—*étudiant révolutionnaire*. Culture might have varied from country to country, but our idealistic dreams and passionate desire for change united student activists around the world. And at the core was our hatred of the Vietnam War.

Our music echoed our rage and became our poetry. It was something new, something better—and as misunderstood by our parents as we were. From the antiwar songs of Country Joe McDonald's "I-Feel-Like-I'm-Fixin'-to-Die Rag" to Jim Morrison and the Doors' "The Unknown Soldier," we listened and we heard and we believed. We knew this was an old man's war that was killing both Vietnamese and unwilling American draftees. America's involvement in the Vietnam War became the epitome of all that was wrong with our parents' generation. Antiwar demonstrations became the rallying point for student activists, young radicals, the left, and the far left and Communist splinter groups.

For that one spring and early summer of 1968, we believed we could change the world both culturally and politically. This was the power of the young. We would demolish old morals and old ideas. We would overcome stereotypes and prejudices, and we would stop the war and topple de Gaulle's repressive French government. We knew without a doubt that we would win, and we wanted at all costs to be part of this. And for a while we were winning. . . . Then it became too difficult to bear the pain and disillusionment.

May 1968 began with the Mouvement du 22 Mars (Movement of March 22) student rebellion at the Université Paris Nanterre. Led by Daniel Cohn-Bendit (also known as Dany le Rouge), the original protest followed the arrest of three young men for bombing an American Express office. In 1968, these offices acted as post offices and banks for U.S. expatriates around the world. What better way to protest the Vietnam War than to bomb something so American?

The protest gained strength when students added complaints about Université Paris Nanterre's crowding and strict dormitory rules. Dany, with his fiery red hair and his fist raised in the air, became an iconic student rebel famous for his inflammatory and impassioned rhetoric. International students studying abroad or those on summer trips listened. Some of us understood Dany's rapid-fire French, some did not, but all were enraptured.

During that early part of May, we sat in friendly cafés and ordered cheap wine or *"un express, s'il vous plaît!"* We had come from all over, including Mexico, Britain, Germany, and America. We had come to Paris to support our French comrades. We Californians with our long unisex hair, hip-hugging bell-bottoms, and peace symbols were the most visible. We were admired for our casual attitudes toward life and free love. We talked late into the night and told stories of last summer in Haight-Ashbury and protests in Berkeley. We discussed the war, sex, music, and drugs while slowly sipping wine or espresso and chain-smoking Gauloises or Gitanes.

We were united in our hatred of the president of France, Charles de Gaulle, and U.S. president Lyndon Johnson. Yes, we knew de Gaulle had been a World War II hero, but that was our parents' war, and it meant nothing to us. We read newspaper reports in *Le Monde* that trivialized our anger and minimized our protests. As we read aloud, we mocked de Gaulle while shouting with laughter at what we considered stupid Gaullist propaganda. When we read aloud articles from the socialist *L'Humanité,* we became quite serious and addressed each other as comrade and talked about how we would change our world. We wondered about the whispers involving Dany Cohn-Bendit and the CIA, but in the end it didn't matter. We argued about fascism and the bourgeoisie and decided that most professors were intellectual whores.

On May 10, we all listened as Cohn-Bendit demanded that all police leave the Latin Quarter and allow us to continue demonstrating. (Paris is a city divided by the river Seine; in 1968 on the Left Bank, in the Latin Quarter, were the radicals, the students, the dreamers, and on the Right Bank the bourgeoisie, the moneyed class, the Gaullists.) According to the police log and as reported in *Le Monde,* the riot of May 10 resulted in: "367 hospitalized of which 251 were police; 720 others hurt and 468 arrested. Cars burned were 60 and 188 others were damaged."

As the national police, Compagnies Républicaines de Sécurité (CRS), fired tear-gas grenades at us, we sang "The Internationale" and "La Marseillaise" and threw paving stones. We laughed and cheered as people in upstairs apartments threw water on us to help counteract the tear gas. Eventually the gas made the air so unbreathable that we were gasping for air. As we retreated, we set fire to our barricades while we chanted *"de Gaulle assassin!"* It was a night of chaos, Molotov cocktails, burned cars, and passion.

What began as a small group of us outside the Sorbonne defending ourselves from police brutality became known as the night of paving stones. We drove the police from the barricades, set cars on fire, and occupied the Sorbonne. We were dirty and hungry and slept on office floors using paper reports as mattresses. But we were never cowed because we knew that our slogan "All power to the imagination" would change France.

This poster announces that the May 1968 events in Paris are only the start of a long struggle. Kate MacMillan states, "This poster gave us hope that we would persevere in our fight for *Égalité! Liberté! Sexualité!*"

When the workers, sympathetic to our cause, called for massive wildcat strikes, we believed together we could and would change France for the better. Their solidarity was embodied by the worker slogans: *An immense force is rising today. The people will win. Liberty for the people.* We were ecstatic when nine million workers joined us in the largest strike Europe has ever known. We watched gleefully as France ground to a halt for almost two weeks.

This poster's slogan, "The police talk to you every night at 8:00 p.m.," refers to nightly news programming on the government-controlled public radio and television stations.

On May 24 we were dismayed by de Gaulle's most recent speech but were heartened by the number of demonstrators joining us as we marched to the Bourse (the French stock exchange). We were a mixture of Trotskyites, anarchists, and revolutionary students, and we sang as we raised the red flag over that Temple of Gold. Parisians lined the streets, as onlookers with their ears glued to their transistor radios listened to the news of the riots. Armed with Molotov cocktails, we marched into the Bourse, shouting, "The Bourse belongs to the workers!" and "Occupy the Bourse!" We cheered as we set it on fire. Then we quickly dispersed and headed back to the Opéra in smaller groups.

Then the CRS attacked us. Blood was spilled and bones were broken and entire blocks of paving stones torn up, trees cut down — streets were devastated. The wreckage and carnage was unbelievable. On May 24 we experienced our first real defeat at the hands of the Gaullist government. Even though he had dual German and French citizenship, Dany Cohn-Bendit was denied entry into France as he returned from Germany. We were shocked and angry to lose this iconic symbol of our resistance when we needed his passionate voice. Dany Cohn-Bendit was not able to legally reenter France for more than a decade.

A few days later, we watched with sadness as thousands marched on the Champs-Élysées supporting de Gaulle. May 1968 lasted a few more tired weeks . . . and then ended with a whimper. We knew it was time to go home to California. Money was in short supply, the bonhomie of the early part of May had evaporated, and all that was left were torn-up paving stones, broken bones, blackened cars, and a lot of memories. It was no longer the great adventure.

Back in this country, we continued to protest the war. There was little if any mainstream media support, but alternative media like the *Berkeley Barb* reported on our demonstrations and often announced them ahead of time. As in Paris, our student numbers grew after each clash with police. Even though we were bringing our protest to the people, American workers did not strike in sympathy. Throughout all of 1968, we continued to protest and march against the war and occupy as many university buildings as possible. However, the time for peaceful rallies was growing short.

Paris taught us that demonstrating against the war was well and good, but success depended on political support. We realized that we needed to become politically active to achieve our goals. We began by supporting the liberal Bobby Kennedy, Eugene McCarthy, or the newly formed Peace and Freedom Party. Most of us could not vote because we were not yet twenty-one, but we were old enough for the draft and old enough to be wounded or killed. Finally, in March 1971, responding to the rallying cry "Old enough to fight, old enough to vote," Congress would pass the Twenty-Sixth Amendment, effectively lowering the voting age to eighteen. For many of us, it would not be soon enough.

As the spring of 1968 wound down, the Democratic convention in Chicago seemed like the best arena for demonstrating our newfound political goals. Like our friends in Paris, we knew we needed the support of sympathetic politicians. As the date came closer, the Yippies, members of the radical, antic Youth International Party, issued their Festival of Life invitation: "We will be in Chicago. Begin preparations now! Chicago is yours! Do it!" Those of us who had been in Paris knew we had to be a part of this. And so we went along with hippies, Yippies, religious and civil rights advocates, intellectuals, and moderates.

Chicago made Paris look civilized. Yes, the CRS had used tear gas in Paris, and some of us had had broken bones and stitches. Yet somehow we knew that it wasn't a personal issue: we, the student protesters, were doing our jobs, and the police were doing theirs. But in Chicago it was a very different story, one that was full of rage and terror. As we fell and bled in the streets, we choked on tear gas and looked into the angry eyes of the police and the scared eyes of the young National Guard soldiers. Chicago was worse than any one of us could ever have imagined.

Later we came to understand that Paris represented a brief moment of renewal and hope. That spring we were filled with optimism, but by the end of summer, that optimism had been smashed by indifference and the unwelcome return of the status quo. In France for a few heady weeks, we had ignited the workers and gathered splinter political groups and intellectuals to our cause. In this country, most Americans were not sympathetic to our antiwar movement, and racial equality was still evolving. Americans were tired of a year of assassinations, riots, and protest demonstrations and wanted a return to law and order. The 1968 election of Richard Nixon was proof of this.

Nineteen sixty-eight is a year that will be forever understood and not understood. Scholarly papers and the news reports of the events contain unsubstantiated descriptions and accounts. Too often the writers and reporters were just observing from the outside rather than inside. Nineteen sixty-eight was our truth and only as each of us experienced it. In the end, some of us kept our activist beliefs and some became apolitical. Some were sent to Vietnam via the draft lottery. Some became famous politicians and authors. Some never made it out alive from the whirlwinds of the time. Some were better for it, and some wished to forget. We braved the world with our idealism, fueled by the power of our beliefs. We were sure we could and would change society. We were forever touched by all that we encountered. We were and will always be *soixante-huitards*.

April
May
June

1968

NIGHTLY NEWS
Elizabeth Partridge

=== SPRING ===

April 4. Dr. King, standing on a hotel balcony, heading out for dinner. A man who is dedicating his whole life to working for civil rights, for all poor people, for peace. Shot dead.

The streets of America erupt in fire, rioting, looting. Black clouds of smoke fill the sky. *Burn, baby, burn.* News cameras switch to home turf for buildings in fiery death throes. Seems like the whole world is burning up.

APRIL 1968
American combat deaths: 1,410
South Vietnamese ally combat deaths: 1,922
Vietnamese enemy combat deaths: 6,653
Vietnamese civilian deaths: 479

That same anger at school like smoldering coals, just waiting to burst into flames. Black kids talking back to teachers, walking out while they're being told to sit back down. A kid slams another kid against a locker. Everybody rushes over, chanting, *Fight, fight, fight,* egging them on. It takes two strong teachers to pull them apart.

Not long till there is combustion. Black and white kids going at each other. *Fight, fight, fight,* and it's on. Keeps happening. Girls start now: slapping, hair-pulling, yanking out earrings. Some boy wades in to stop it. Other boys rush in, throwing textbooks, slugging, kicking each other. Meant to hurt, bring blood, break teeth.

Whenever I hear *Fight, fight, fight* echo down the hallway, I turn and run.

MAY 1968
American combat deaths: 2,169
South Vietnamese ally combat deaths: 3,467
Vietnamese enemy combat deaths: 12,543
Vietnamese civilian deaths: 568

June 5: Stay up late for live election coverage on the eleven o'clock news. Finally the votes are tallied: Bobby Kennedy has won California's Democratic primary. Crowd makes way for him to get to the podium. It's late, and he looks tired. Says it's time to move in a different direction.

We want Bobby, people chant, packed in shoulder to shoulder. *We want Bobby.*

Kennedy smiles, weary, flashes a peace sign, and slips out the back corridor, through the hotel kitchen.

Shots, yelling, screaming, and Kennedy's down on the floor. Someone presses a rosary into his hand. *Is everybody okay?* he whispers. *Don't lift me.*

Doctors try to save him, but he doesn't make it. Shot dead.

Those church bells tolling in my head, mournful and low, drowning out thinking, leaving an empty place inside. Just won't quit clanging.

JUNE 1968
American combat deaths: 1,146
South Vietnamese ally combat deaths: 1,974
Vietnamese enemy combat deaths: 8,168
Vietnamese civilian deaths: 363

THE DEATH OF THE DREAM

The Assassinations of the Reverend Dr. Martin Luther King Jr. and Robert F. Kennedy

KEKLA MAGOON

On April 4, 1968, Robert F. Kennedy stood on a makeshift stage in the middle of a poor black neighborhood in Indianapolis, Indiana. As he was ushered toward the microphone, he turned to one of the organizers and asked, "Do they know about Martin Luther King?" The man's answer: No.

Resigned to the inevitable, Senator Kennedy turned to the microphone. He began: "I have some very sad news for all of you, and I think sad news for all of our fellow citizens, and people who love peace all over the world, and that is that Martin Luther King was shot and was killed tonight in Memphis, Tennessee."

Cries of grief, anguish, and shock rose up from the crowd. The people who had gathered to hear Senator Kennedy make this campaign stop reeled from the impact of his unexpected words. Having received the news shortly before his appearance, Senator Kennedy had been advised to cancel his speech. The Indianapolis police insisted that they would be unable to protect him in the event that violence broke out in the community. To his credit, Senator Kennedy did not take the easy out. Instead he attempted to offer comfort to a group of citizens who would be among the most affected by the day's tragedy.

"In this difficult day, in this difficult time for the United States, it is perhaps well to ask what kind of a nation we are and what direction we want to move in. For those of you who are black—considering the evidence evidently is that there were white people who were responsible—you can be filled with bitterness, and with hatred, and a desire for revenge. We can move in that direction as a country, in greater polarization—black people amongst blacks, and white amongst whites, filled with hatred toward one another.

"Or we can make an effort, as Martin Luther King did, to understand and to comprehend, and replace that violence, that stain of bloodshed that has spread across our land, with an effort to understand, compassion, and love."

The speech lasted just under five minutes—brief, spontaneous remarks that no doubt differed significantly from the message he had intended to impart that evening. Senator Kennedy's remarks are credited with helping maintain calm in Indianapolis that night. In other major cities around the country—Baltimore, Chicago, Detroit, Los Angeles, Newark, New York, Philadelphia, Seattle—riots did break out as black Americans learned the tragic news of Dr. King's murder.

That week, Dr. King had been in Memphis supporting a local sanitation workers' strike. At around four p.m., he and his staff left his second-floor room at the Lorraine Motel. As they walked across the outdoor balcony toward the stairs, a single rifle shot rang out. The bullet struck Dr. King in the neck, causing massive bleeding. He fell. His aides surrounded him, trying to stop the bleeding. Some pointed across the street, toward the building where the shot had come from. He was rushed to the hospital, where he was pronounced dead. With his murder, a great light of hope for black Americans was extinguished, never to be rekindled.

• • •

The investigation into his death would ultimately return a single sus-pect: James Earl Ray, a petty criminal who had escaped from prison the previous year and disappeared. Ray's political leanings made him a staunch segregationist, and his motive for shooting the well-known civil rights leader stemmed from these beliefs. After the shooting, he pulled another disappearing act. Ray successfully eluded law enforce-ment for two months before he was apprehended using a known alias at the London airport.

For many, Dr. King represented hope and the promise that justice, equality, and opportunity lay just around the corner. To lose him — particularly in such a violent and intentional manner — was to lose faith in the movement he had spearheaded. After decades of stead-fast commitment to civil disobedience and passive resistance, people's sorrow and rage boiled over.

Black Americans were no strangers to discontent, to disappoint-ment, to sorrow, to rage. They were no strangers to fighting for change. This drive had been passed down through the generations, from the enslaved black people who rebelled against the plantation owners who systematically stripped them of humanity to the abolitionists and free blacks whose advocacy helped liberate their people. It had been passed to the Reconstruction-era activists who negotiated for representation and reparations post-emancipation, giving rise to white supremacist backlash in the form of Jim Crow and the Ku Klux Klan. It had been passed to the turn-of-the-twentieth-century activists who fought for opportunities in education and advancement, and passed again to the civil rights movement leaders of the 1950s and early 1960s, who had demonstrated for over a decade and earned the victories of dismantling legal segregation and seeing the Voting Rights Act and Civil Rights Act passed.

At the beginning of 1968, these most recent victories felt like a pinnacle of achievement, and yet leaders like Dr. King recognized that they were only laying the groundwork for lasting social and political change. Senator Kennedy's remarks may have brought a sense of calm and comfort to the people of Indianapolis that night, but his words merely skimmed the surface of a larger social upheaval that was already under way.

The Rise of Black Power

The reality for black Americans in 1968 was that not enough had changed as a result of civil rights organizing. Dr. King's assassination codified a growing dissatisfaction among young black activists. The promises of the civil rights era that should have been coming to fruition instead seemed to be fading. The nation was caught in a military conflict overseas that threatened to further exacerbate tensions at home. Black teenagers who had been active in civil rights movement protests felt deeply uncomfortable about the prospect of military service. They felt they were being asked to march beneath an American flag overseas to defend a set of freedoms that were not being extended to them back home. As the boxer Muhammad Ali famously put it, "Why should they ask me to put on a uniform and go ten thousand miles from home and drop bombs and bullets on brown people in Vietnam while so-called Negro people in Louisville are treated like dogs and denied simple human rights?"

A similar discontent had plagued their fathers a generation earlier. In World War II, black units were often sent to the front lines and were often first onto the battlefield. They served proudly, but returned home to a glaring inconsistency. This great war of the mid-twentieth century had supposedly been about securing freedom and democracy for the world, yet black Americans were second-class citizens. This disparity was now thrown into sharper relief, and black servicemen's frustrations helped drive the civil rights movement that would unfold over the subsequent two decades. By the dawn of the Vietnam era, young black men of draft age (eighteen to twenty-five) were all too aware that they were being asked to fight a war abroad on the promise of a freedom that was being denied to them at home.

By 1968, young black people had reached a fever pitch of frustration with the slow process of change. Their entire lives had been defined by this struggle, and what did they have to show for it? Despite legal progress, the nation rapidly self-corrected to maintain its comfort zone of white privilege. The systems and laws that had been formally dismantled by the destruction of Jim Crow were quickly replaced with de facto segregation. Black Americans struggled against intractable economic disadvantage. Gerrymandering and disenfranchisement rendered voting rights all but meaningless. Police brutality was rampant throughout the country. The denial of education and opportunities continued.

Thanks to the teachings of Malcolm X, there was a growing awareness of the systemic nature of racism. There would be no quick fix for all that was wrong with race relations in America, and young black people in particular sought new ways to fight.

Huey Newton and Bobby Seale founded the Black Panther Party for Self-Defense in Oakland, California, in the fall of 1966. The Panthers' Ten-Point Platform and Program outlined their demands for racial equality and justice, and they followed it up with community organizing activities that ranged from political education classes to weapons training to service projects. They functioned as a political party, seeking to put progressive candidates in office at local and national levels. The Panthers operated community service programs that took care of people's immediate needs: food programs, schools, health clinics, legal aid, and community policing. The party articulated and then began to enact the most significant steps that must be taken to ensure "land, bread, housing, education, clothing, justice and peace" for all Americans.

The Panthers drew followers because they tapped into the feeling that the movement wasn't accomplishing enough fast enough and that waiting for the powers that be to take action might not actually move the needle. Black people hungered to take real, concrete action — beyond marching and protesting — to effect long-term change in their communities. Between 1967 and 1970, the Black Panther Party opened chapters in forty cities around the country.

This transition to self-defense (broadly defined) was a necessary shift and one that was happening anyway, but Dr. King's death became a catalyst for something that might otherwise have been a slower burn.

The Challenge of Moderation

Dr. King advocated faith, persistence, and patience as the keys to civil rights progress. As such, his own devotion to nonviolent passive resistance is often oversimplified. His death occurred in a moment when he had begun to reconsider the reality of what long-term progress would actually look like. He would likely never have come around to the Black Panther Party's way of thinking regarding armed self-defense; however, he grew closer to their position on systemic change and long-term community organizing. In the days preceding his death, he was in Memphis supporting a sanitation workers' strike. Much like the Montgomery Bus Boycott earlier in the decade, this strike would leverage the power of many workers coming together to impact the economic systems governing their lives. This practice stands among the strongest and most effective styles of protest, and slight shifts in his rhetoric and actions made powerful people regard Dr. King as increasingly dangerous.

As Senator Kennedy attempted to calm and comfort the people of Indianapolis that night, he naturally pointed to the difficult emotions accompanying the struggle: "For those of you who are black and are tempted to be filled with hatred and distrust at the injustice of such an act, against all white people, I can only say that I feel in my own heart the same kind of feeling. I had a member of my family killed . . . by a white man." It was the only time Robert Kennedy referred publicly to his grief and anger over the loss of his brother, President John F. Kennedy, who had been assassinated five years earlier.

Knowingly or not, Senator Kennedy then echoed a sentiment that Dr. King had expressed in his final speech in Memphis the previous night, about the difficult times ahead, saying: "We've had difficult times in the past; we will have difficult times in the future. It is not the end of violence; it is not the end of lawlessness; it is not the end of disorder."

The Other Shoe Drops

As he spoke about Dr. King's assassination that night, Senator Kennedy had no way of knowing that almost exactly two months later, he would suffer a similar fate. On June 5, he stood in the ballroom of the Ambassador Hotel in Los Angeles, where he jubilantly accepted a victory in the California presidential primary. The win put him one giant step closer to securing the Democratic Party nomination for president of the United States. He was expected to campaign throughout the summer and fall, and run against the likely Republican nominee, then senator Richard M. Nixon, in November.

After acknowledging the win in California shortly after midnight, Senator Kennedy left the podium. His security personnel escorted him, his wife, and his aides through the kitchen to avoid getting mobbed by the exuberant crowd. A man rushed forward with a gun. He fired, striking the senator three times and wounding several other people with errant bullets as he was wrestled to the ground. Sirhan Bishara Sirhan, a Palestinian with Jordanian citizenship, was immediately apprehended on site. He later confessed to the shooting and claimed his actions were inspired by disagreement over U.S. policies toward Palestine.

Senator Kennedy was rushed to the hospital, where he died in the early morning of June 6. Once again, the nation fell into mourning. So much felt up in the air for people; between the escalating Vietnam conflict and the unrelenting backlash against civil rights organizing, Americans of all races struggled to make sense of the times.

A Generational Divide

Senator Kennedy's presidential campaign arose amid a sea of political turmoil. Civil rights and racial equality represented merely a portion of the pressing concerns affecting Americans. The question of U.S. involvement in the war in Vietnam further polarized the nation.

The challenges of managing a costly and controversial war took a toll on the government. Sitting president Lyndon B. Johnson had announced in March 1968 that he would neither seek nor accept a second term as U.S. president. Other than Senator Kennedy, the lead candidates in the Democratic primary included Senator Eugene McCarthy and Vice President Hubert Humphrey. The dividing line between the two, for many voters, was their position on Vietnam. McCarthy appealed to the young voters who stood staunchly against the war, while Humphrey emerged as the "establishment" candidate, whose election would assure the Johnson administration's policies regarding the conflict continued. Thus, a generational divide defined the political landscape in black and white communities alike.

Senator Kennedy had been a somewhat more unifying presence amid the fray. He was "establishment" enough to satisfy some of the elders and antiwar enough to capture the youth vote as well. He also emerged as the favorite among black voters, as he seemed most likely to continue the drive to assure civil rights for all. It was widely believed at the time that he had a very good chance of winning not only the

Democratic primary but the general presidential election. His untimely death plunged the Democratic Party into chaos.

Senator Kennedy's support base included many young white college students who were actively protesting U.S. involvement in the war in Vietnam. These students came largely from middle- and upper-middle-class backgrounds. They operated from within a sense of entitlement that black protesters and working-class whites lacked. White antiwar activists protested the morality of the war and the morality of a draft, but without the added layer of actual inequality and injustice facing black people of the same age.

Students for a Democratic Society (SDS) emerged as a lead organization in the antiwar movement. Founded at the University of Michigan in 1960 as a new iteration of a student labor organization, SDS issued its manifesto, the Port Huron Statement, which critiqued a variety of U.S. government policies. Unfortunately, their attitudes and behaviors read as selfish and petulant to their elders, many of whom grew up during the Great Depression and fought in World War II. By contrast, SDS activists were young privileged white men with every opportunity available to them, including the choice to defer conscription to pursue higher education. Their black activist contemporaries decried their lack of connection to the more pressing issues of the moment, like civil rights and racism. Instead of using their voices of privilege to weigh in on those debates, the SDS paid lip service to the cause of civil rights while promoting their own agenda.

As a candidate for president, Senator McCarthy's platform most closely reflected the concerns of SDS and the student antiwar movement, yet—despite his track record of supporting these issues in the Senate—his campaign lacked a significant commitment to civil rights organizing. Senator Kennedy had previously served as attorney general under President John F. Kennedy. He had also witnessed and participated in the government's response to civil rights. Certainly civil rights advocates argued that he could be doing more for the cause, but he remained sympathetic and was regarded by many as the best hope of making continued progress. The loss of Kennedy undercut the country's ability to heal from the generational rifts plaguing both races.

The Lightning Rod

In a defining moment like 1968, even seemingly small challenges can create ripple effects that might change the course of a nation. And the deaths of Dr. King and Senator Kennedy were not small challenges. Taken separately, each death was a national tragedy. Taken together, these successive assassinations represented a catastrophic loss of visionary leadership (King) and of the power and position to enact it (Kennedy).

King and Kennedy were still relatively young men when they died. They stood in a position straddling the cusp of two generations. They shared the vision of the younger generation coming up but still had sufficient respect for established institutions to operate within the structures of society. For better and worse, they played by the rules. These were two men who would have been able to continue to walk the halls of government without setting buildings on fire.

As a result of these losses, progressive leadership necessarily pivoted to the next generation—a generation so preoccupied with inspiring change and disrupting the establishment that they were unable or unwilling to invest in the establishment at that moment.

In an ideal scenario, both strategies of change would have continued in tandem. To enact lasting civil rights change, the country needed a radical youth element like the Panthers to emerge and challenge the status quo. We arguably also needed a radical youth protest engine like SDS to draw attention to the administration's policies on Vietnam and turn public opinion away from deepening the conflict. But these younger leaders' approaches often skewed too radical to make headway within the existing system.

It did not help matters that, following each assassination, rumors of conspiracy abounded. Just like with the assassinations of President John F. Kennedy and civil rights leader Malcolm X earlier in the decade, the deaths of the Reverend Dr. King and Robert F. Kennedy seemed awfully convenient for their political opponents. The official investigation in each case returned the same conclusion: this murder was the work of a lone gunman. Both suspects were apprehended, tried, and convicted. Yet many people persist in believing that there may be more to the story in one or both cases. These two assassinations occurred at such pivotal moments. Coincidence? From this place in history, it is impossible to know for sure what was going on in the minds and hearts of the shooters or if they had help or support in conducting these acts of treachery. What does remain certain is the impact that the deaths of Martin Luther King Jr. and Robert F. Kennedy had on the country. They were shots heard round the world.

THE WRONG SIDE OF HISTORY

My Family's Racist Reaction to Dr. Martin Luther King Jr.'s Assassination

LABAN CARRICK HILL

On April 4, 1968, I was seven years old. This was the day Martin Luther King Jr. was assassinated in Memphis. I didn't know who King was. His name had never come up in the presence of the children in our family. So this was the day I learned not just who he was but also how much he was hated by many whites in Memphis, including my own family. My mother, father, older sister, and I were down in Memphis for our school's spring break. We lived year-round in a suburb of New York City, but the rest of our family lived in and around Memphis. My family returned to Memphis almost every vacation. Memphis was home. It was where everyone had been born, except for me.

When we visited Memphis, we always stayed with my mother's older brother, Uncle Ben, and Aunt Emmaline, and their children, Bess and Lane. They lived in a large mansion on Yates Road on the east side of the city. Before he turned thirty, Uncle Ben had made his first million constructing Holiday Inns around the country. By the time of King's assassination, he owned nearly a hundred of these motels and was building more every day. He reigned over his home like a despot on the edge of explosion. My mother worshipped the ground her older brother walked on, and he had the kind of stature that demanded worship. Uncle Ben was a massive man, six feet five inches tall, with a booming voice and demeanor not unlike Big Daddy's in Tennessee Williams's *Cat on a Hot Tin Roof*. He was cartoonish in his size and violence. He was not reluctant to give me a hard smack when he felt I was out of line. My sister, Susan, and I tended to stay out of sight of the adults as much as possible.

When King was murdered, my family was on the wrong side of history. They were white Southerners who benefited immensely from Jim Crow. They believed that *Brown v. Board of Education*, the 1964 Civil Rights Act, and the 1965 Voting Rights Act were not just wrong and unconstitutional, but against the natural order of humankind, and therefore evil. My family had spent an enormous amount of time and energy doing what they would have called "protecting" me from the "dangerous" black population. We never ventured into black neighborhoods or interacted with African Americans who were not in service positions.

One hot summer day, when I was four and we were living in the suburbs of Philadelphia, my mom left Susan and me in the care of our black maid. The woman, whose name I cannot remember, decided she needed to go home for some reason, so she took us on the trolley into the inner city of North Philadelphia. When we stepped off the trolley, Susan and I were in a world we had never seen and could not have imagined. Our world was a place where everyone had a lawn and lived in stand-alone homes. This new place was noisy with traffic. All kinds of stores lined the streets. Since I couldn't read, all I remember was a kaleidoscope of colors and sounds—brilliant blues and yellows and reds. The sidewalks were crowded with people, but a people I had hardly ever seen. These people were mostly black. It was exciting for Susan and me. We still talk about it today. We had lunch in the lady's kitchen in a second-floor apartment that was bright with sunlight. The smells were strange, heavy with exhaust and grease. By late afternoon, we returned home. As we shared with our mom the wonders of the day, her face hardened, etched into stone. We never saw the maid again. That was the extent of my experience with other races during my childhood.

So on that April 4 when King was assassinated, the entire family gathered around the dinner table. Normally the children would have eaten at a kids' table, away from the adults. Not this day, when around dinnertime, the telephone started ringing, and the house exploded into a fury and agitation. Emelia, Uncle Ben's African-American maid, left abruptly for the bus in the middle of dinner preparations. Later, we heard that city buses had been canceled. I wondered if Emelia was able to get home, but none of the adults seemed interested in checking to see. Since Emelia was gone, Aunt Emmaline had to take charge in the kitchen. That's why we all ended up gathering at the dining-room table, children and adults alike. I distinctly remember my grandparents, Granny and Poppa, being there because Granny had had a couple of bourbon-and-branch-waters, which had loosened her tongue. She referred to the Reverend Dr. Martin Luther King Jr. as "that n—er." The general consensus was that his death was going to "stir things up" and that "those n—ers" would make it difficult for them, meaning people like my family.

Aunt Emmaline bemoaned the fact that Emelia probably wouldn't come to work for a while. Uncle Ben responded, "Well, she won't get paid, then." My cousin Lane, two years older than me, volunteered that John, the African-American man who mowed their lawn, probably wouldn't come the next day, even though he was scheduled. At this point, a litany of how King's death would inconvenience the adults erupted around the table. There was no sense of sorrow, regret, or mourning in their words for King, his family, or African Americans.

I laid my head on my pillow that night afraid that we might be killed in our beds. The conversation around the table had turned toward fears of riots. I imagined African Americans marauding through our neighborhoods, burning homes and killing. Nothing that my parents, aunt and uncle, or grandparents said alleviated my fears.

Who King was, I still didn't understand. I knew he was a black man who was important to black people and who white people didn't like, but I knew there were a lot of black men — as well as black women — who the adults in my family didn't like. In fact, very rarely did I hear a family member say the offensive and demeaning description that a particular African American was "a good n—er." I knew that the N-word was bad. I had been told that at school. I had learned it in school up North, but I also don't seem to have been outraged by my family's casual use of the word. I just didn't know. That was all I could ascertain at that point. In Memphis, we socialized only with white people, and the only time I encountered a black person was as a domestic service person. The same could be said about where we lived in New York — the white suburb of Scarsdale. There were no black people at my school besides one janitor, the only adult in the building whom we called by his first name.

In my family, there were two ways that African Americans were talked about: either blacks were dangerous and threatening or they were like overgrown children. Poppa used to tell a story about a black man who worked around his house and store when my mother was little. No one seemed to know his real name. Poppa, Granny, Uncle Ben, and my mom called him Rabbit, as if in some way, as a black man, he was incapable in earning the dignity of a human name; he had to be called by an animal name. This was in stark contrast to the dogs around the house that had names like Buddy and Fred — human names.

Poppa's story was one about the supposed innocence of Rabbit, but it really tells a story of the exploitation of blacks by the white-controlled Memphis government. Every once in a while, Rabbit would be picked up by the police for drunkenness and be housed in the city jail, which was across the street from Gethsemane Episcopal Church, the church my grandparents attended.

On Sundays, Poppa would arrive at church with two cartons of cigarettes from his grocery store. Rabbit would shout through the barred windows of the jail, and Poppa would cross the street and hand him the cigarettes through the bars. Rabbit would usually be imprisoned for lack of bail money for a month or so. During that time, he and his fellow African-American inmates would be put to work on the roads. Every spring Rabbit and other disenfranchised African-American men would be "rounded up" and put on the work crew into the summer. Poppa never talked about the injustice that Rabbit experienced. Instead, he would laugh and tell his story about how he was one of the good whites because he helped out Rabbit with a couple of cartons of cigarettes.

The day after King's assassination, I heard Uncle Ben complaining about the *Memphis Press-Scimitar,* the local newspaper. He called to cancel his subscription because the paper had featured King above the fold while placing the article about calling up the National Guard to protect the city below the fold. In his mind, King's assassination was secondary to the dangers of rioting African Americans who might cross from Orange Mound, the black, segregated part of town, into East Memphis. The irony is that Memphis didn't erupt into violence like many other cities in the United States during what came to be known as Holy Week Uprising. This was especially surprising because King had been in Memphis to support the "I Am a Man" sanitation workers' strike. Nevertheless, we were banned from leaving the mansion's fenced-in yard.

On this day, a kernel began to germinate in me. There was something not right about what Uncle Ben had said. As a seven-year-old, I did not have the words to explain it, but I knew somewhere deep down in my soul that what King had done was not wrong. I knew violence, and King was about peace. I knew violence in my family. I had been the victim of that violence in the middle of the night when I had been plucked out of bed and thrown against a wall from some supposed infraction earlier in the day. Even at seven years old, I sensed that my uncle Ben and by extension my entire family had little credibility. I didn't know what to do with this unformed realization, but from this day it would grow.

A year to the day after King was assassinated, my grandfather Joe, my father's father, died in Tipton County Hospital about forty miles north of Memphis. His death came three months after a teenage African-American child was murdered in my grandfather's laundromat with my grandfather's gun. A group of African-American teenage boys were on their way back from the homecoming game of the segregated high school. At that time of night, my grandfather's twenty-four-hour, "blacks-only" laundromat was the only place in town that an African American could get a Coca-Cola. The boys put their money in the machine, and the machine didn't deliver a Coke. They rocked the machine to try to make the nickel fall into the proper slot. That night my grandfather had hired a drinking friend of his to be a guard and had given him his gun. The man came out of the back room and shot one boy to death and wounded another. When my grandfather died in his hospital bed, my uncle Melvin and my grandmother Zoelette claimed they had witnessed the mother of the dead boy enter my grandfather's room just before he died. An investigation was made, but no charges were filed. For decades, my family believed that the mother of the murdered teen had killed my grandfather for revenge on the first anniversary of King's assassination.

I never believed it. I knew the kinds of stories my family could make up to justify their racism. For my grandmother, uncles, and father, Grandfather Joe had to be a victim, not a victimizer. To this end, he had to die not from natural causes but at the hand of an African American. I had no proof then, but I knew this was myth, not truth.

Years later, I spent a few months investigating my family's claim. What I discovered was: first, my grandfather had died of pneumonia, cirrhosis, hepatitis, and several other ailments at once. He had been at death's door for days. Second, the woman who was accused wasn't the mother of the murdered child. She actually had nothing to do with the families of the children shot, except she had the same last name. In truth, she was the wife of the president of the local chapter of the NAACP and was the only African-American registered nurse in the hospital. The hospital had just been forced to rehire her after her successful four-year-long discrimination suit in federal court. She was the last person who would have wanted to kill my grandfather. She had bigger fish to fry. Nevertheless, the myth of my grandfather's death was held dear to my grandparents' and parents' generation.

Just four years after King's assassination, my parents divorced, and my mother, sister, and I returned to Memphis permanently. A few months later, I picked up the afternoon paper route for the *Memphis Press-Scimitar*. First off, I tried to sign Uncle Ben up for a subscription. His response wasn't just to say no to me, but to pick up the phone and call the newspaper's executive editor to spit a stream of vitriol at him about the paper's coverage of the King assassination. For Uncle Ben, time never passed. By the time we moved, however, I knew who King was, knew how important he was to America, and knew how wrong my uncle Ben and other members of my family were. Times had truly changed between 1968 and 1972. It was a mighty river of change that couldn't be stopped. The Memphis Public Schools had finally desegregated after eighteen years of resistance. The "colored" water fountains were a thing of legend. Most of my family had also learned a hard lesson—not to stop being racist, but rather to keep their mouths shut. Then they could never be called racists. *Being* a racist wasn't the problem; being *called* a racist was.

Susan and I were enrolled in all-white private schools. Diversity in our school was represented by the Jewish sisters who attended, and they had a rough time of it. Even though I had already been having doubts about my family, I did not really begin to articulate this until I realized that Uncle Ben was a bully. My grandparents and other relatives on both sides had a hidden vein of contempt for African Americans that was rarely revealed, and only in private. Their anger struck me as wrong. As a preteen, I still could not express exactly what made me feel injustice. The language would take decades to master. Still, I distanced myself from them and began to find heroes in black culture, the exact opposite of the heroes my family and my school idolized. I loved the blaxploitation movies and would ride the bus downtown to the black movie theaters to watch movies like *Uptown Saturday Night* and *Superfly*. I had all of Bill Cosby's comedy records and Isaac Hayes's *Shaft* record. My mother thought I was weird, but she didn't stop me.

Around this time, something happened that changed my life. We lived in a segregated apartment complex down Yates Avenue from Uncle Ben. When I was in the seventh grade, Isaac Hayes bought a piece of the King Plantation and built a mansion just past Uncle Ben's mansion. He was the first African American to move into the neighborhood. My best friend, Crit, lived across the street. We would stand in the woods beside the entrance to Hayes's property, and we'd watch these incredible black men and women get in and out of black limousines in their floor-length black leather coats and black or gold platform shoes. We dreamed of dressing like them. Of somehow being them.

That year, I ended up going to the school prom wearing three-inch platform shoes, red plaid elephant bell-bottom pants, a bright-red wide-lapelled sport coat, and a butterfly bow tie. I thought I was the height of cool and took my lessons where I could. I never missed *Soul Train* on Saturday afternoons and would practice my moves in front of the television. I wanted to dance like James Brown. Get down!

In 1978, ten years after King's assassination, I moved back to

New York. I was lucky enough to get a job working in Harlem and the South Bronx (what my white family and many others would call "the ghetto"). I would walk from block to block in both neighborhoods, talking to people and gathering information about laundry detergent sales for a market research firm. My own family's horrible connection to laundries wasn't lost on me. That summer, I experienced the wonder and beauty of these communities as well as the tragedy. It was strange to walk the streets of a community my family had taught me was dangerous and evil and to then discover the humanity there. It was there, in Harlem and the South Bronx, that I was introduced to hip-hop. It was there that I really began to understand that the poisonous consequences of racism harm not only African Americans but everyone—the victim and the victimizer. Ralph Ellison once wrote, "Whatever else the true American is, he is also somehow Black." Ellison's words reveal just how much we cannot walk away and ignore the past and the present. We are too interconnected. We cannot just repair the past, but must repair the present as well.

GYM CROW

How Student Protesters Halted the Construction of a Segregated Gym

JENNIFER ANTHONY

Columbia University, New York City, April 9, 1968. It was an unseasonably warm spring day, and about to grow even hotter. More than 1,100 people were filing into Saint Paul's Chapel to honor Martin Luther King Jr., who had been assassinated five days earlier.

One of the mourners was Mark Rudd, a junior at Columbia.

Rudd handed out leaflets to people as they walked into the chapel. The leaflets told how Columbia mistreated its minority employees, how the university had evicted thousands of residents — most of them black or Latino — from Morningside Heights single-room-occupancy buildings and apartments, and how the university had stolen land from a public park to build a gym with one grand entrance in the front for predominantly white Columbia students and another entrance in the back for Harlem residents, who were predominantly black.

Rudd sat quietly as the university president called the mourners to worship. He and the other attendees listened to addresses from the chaplain and interfaith counselors.

They listened as a rector from nearby Harlem read selections from Dr. King's writings and speeches. Most held hands and joined

in, reverently, to the singing of "We Shall Overcome." Martin Luther
King Jr. had fought for nonviolent resistance. He had promoted change
through peaceful demonstrations and encouraged students to use nonviolent methods during their protests.

There was a time when Rudd had been an idealist and a pacifist.
But he had changed. He had returned recently from a trip to Cuba, and
the trip had him "fired up with revolutionary fervor."

Now the service was making Rudd's blood boil. He was determined
to speak up.

Rudd slid from the pew and headed to the speaker's platform. He
grabbed the microphone. He looked out over the crowd. Most of the
faces were white like his. Later, he would admit that he was afraid. How
would the crowd react?

Someone — Rudd didn't know who — had hurried to click off the
microphone. Rudd called out Columbia University, saying that it was
"committed to a policy of racism" and that university officials such as
Provost David Truman and President Grayson Kirk were "committing a
moral outrage against Dr. King's memory."

For about a month, Rudd had served as chair of Columbia's chapter
of Students for a Democratic Society, or SDS, a national organization
that had chapters on campuses throughout the United States. That day
at the memorial, he spoke on behalf of SDS, which opposed capitalism
and spoke out against the university's support of the Vietnam War.
Rudd was also concerned about how the university was encroaching
upon neighboring communities.

With no microphone, Rudd raised his voice. The university "steals
lands from the people of Harlem," he shouted. "We will therefore protest against this obscenity."

As Rudd and his fellow SDS members left the chapel feeling angrier
and more determined than ever, congregants admonished them, calling out "Shame," "Blasphemy," and "This is a church."

University president Grayson Kirk watched the protesters leave. He had stood to one side during the singing of "We Shall Overcome." He hadn't held hands or joined. Kirk's blood was boiling, too. He had put Rudd and a few others on discretionary probation for violating a rule about indoor demonstrations a month before, and now Rudd was causing trouble again.

The Morningside Heights campus looked out over Harlem, at the time the largest black inner-city neighborhood in America, where nearly a quarter of the population relied on welfare and more than seven thousand residents had been evicted from Columbia-controlled properties. And yet members of another campus organization, the Student Afro-American Society (SAS), had not been formally invited to the memorial service.

In the two weeks that followed the memorial, SDS members strategized about their next steps. The time for peaceful protests was over. On April 12, one of the SDS committees voted to approve a series of demonstrations and disruptions later that month.

Rudd wrote an open letter to the university president that he called "Reply to Uncle Grayson." He declared that the letter was "the opening shot in a war of liberation." The letter warned Grayson that SDS tactics were about to change. "Up against the wall," Rudd warned Grayson. "This is a stick-up."

Noon, April 23. Rudd stood amid a crowd of roughly five hundred people gathered at the sundial, a raised platform on campus and one of the highest points on the island of Manhattan. Fittingly, the fortress-like buildings that loomed over low-lying Harlem stood on the same ground where Americans had fought an early battle of the Revolutionary War.

Rudd and his fellow SDS members were prepared to fight. They wanted Columbia to end its ties with the Institute for Defense Analyses (IDA), which they argued was advancing weapons research that contributed to the Vietnam War. They wanted to reverse such policies as disallowing indoor protests. They wanted to stop the university's plans to build a gymnasium with separate doors for Columbia students and Harlem residents.

But this time, Rudd's SDS members weren't fighting alone. Members of the SAS, led by sophomore Cicero Wilson, stood beside them at the sundial. Rudd had met with Wilson at midnight the night before. The two were introduced by an SDS member who played in a soul music band with Wilson.

Wilson and his SAS members were also angry about the university's racist policies and the construction of the gym. Over the years, Columbia University had spread like an octopus, reaching its tentacles farther into the black community. Referring to the limited access that Harlem residents would have to the gymnasium, they distributed a flier that cried, "Stop Columbia's Gym Crow."

This was a momentous day. It was the first time that Columbia's black and white students had formed an alliance against the university's administration. Cicero Wilson addressed the mostly white crowd of protesters. "This is Harlem Heights, not Morningside Heights," Wilson said. What would whites do if someone tried to seize their land? he wanted to know.

The demonstrators were energized. "Did we come here to talk, or did we come here to go to Low [Library]?" yelled an SDS member. "IDA MUST GO!" they chanted.

The protesters broke into a run. They raced across campus, pushing past the counterdemonstrators who held up signs. One of these signs demanded "Send Rudd Back to Cuba!" Another read "Order Is Peace."

At Low Library, the protesters found the doors locked and campus guards standing at the building's security entrance. Rudd scrambled atop a garbage can, trying to figure out what to do next. Someone shouted, "Let's head to the gym, let's go to the gym site!"

Protesters surged toward the gymnasium site, where construction was under way. Rudd followed.

The protest was taking on a life of its own. The sounds of wailing police sirens and rumbling bulldozers filled the air. Protesters had started tearing down the chain-link fence surrounding the construction site. A fight between the cops and the protesters had broken out. One policeman grabbed a demonstrator. Other protesters jumped on top of the officer, shoving him aside. Another officer rushed to help, and the protesters jumped him, too. Another officer reached for his firearm as he tussled with a black SAS member. The student grabbed the officer's thumb and twisted it back. Sophomore Fred Wilson (white and no relation to Cicero Wilson) fought with the police, and they arrested him, charging him with two felonies and two misdemeanors.

Rudd climbed up on a hillock of dirt and called for protesters to regroup at the sundial. He had a plan. A big plan. He told them that they would start by "taking a hostage." Chanting and clapping, about three hundred SAS and SDS leaders headed to Hamilton Hall, where the dean's offices were located.

There in Hamilton Hall's lobby stood the acting dean, Henry Coleman, with the university's chief security officer, William Kahn, at his side. The angry and shaken dean had inadvertently played into the protesters' hands. Protesters trapped the two in the dean's office, not allowing them to leave until the dean had agreed to drop the charges against Fred Wilson.

The excitement over holding a building and two faculty members as hostages energized Rudd and his fellow SDS members. They had learned from black protesters that nonviolent resistance requires imagination.

In 1960, for example, four young black men had staged a sit-in at a "whites only" lunch counter at a Woolworth's, vowing to return every day with more people until they were served.

The Columbia protesters settled in. They strung red balloons and crepe paper across the lobby's white plaster pillars and along its walls. They taped antiwar posters throughout the hall. They posted pictures of prominent black civil rights activists such as Stokely Carmichael and Malcolm X and famous Communist leaders such as Vladimir Lenin and Che Guevara to walls and columns. A Che Guevara placard read, "In revolution, one wins or dies." Sympathizers brought them bananas, oranges, and apples.

But it was one thing for white protesters to talk about revolution and another to enact it. It was one thing to talk about racism and another to live it.

That evening, SAS committee members and representatives of the black community came together and spoke their minds.

Like the white protesters, the black protesters opposed the gymnasium construction. But their concerns about the university's treatment of black students and their experience at the school ran deeper. These weren't experiences that happened to other students. These were issues that had happened or might happen to them—that they had likely experienced firsthand. One protester, for example, shared how he and his black friends would get called racial slurs when they walked past the school's row of fraternities.

To the black protesters, the SDS members and their followers were indecisive. SDS would make decisions, then undo them. "SDS can stand on the side and support us . . . but the black students and the Harlem community will be the ones in the vanguard," said Cicero Wilson. The black students would lead the way.

That evening, four new faces showed up at the meeting: H. Rap Brown, a leader of the Student Nonviolent Coordinating Committee

(SNCC, known as "Snick"), along with three bodyguards. When Brown addressed the attendees, he was thankful but firm. He and his compatriots did not want white Columbia students speaking for them. "I'd like to tell you that the Harlem community is now here and we want to thank you for taking the first steps in this struggle. The black community is taking over," Brown said.

The black students and community members stayed up that night, talking and planning how to make their own voices heard in non-violent ways. They had had enough of white people speaking for them.

Before sunrise the next morning, SAS leaders approached the white students in Hamilton Hall. As campus Episcopal chaplain William Starr described it, the SAS leaders said to the white students, "People are hanging out in the halls and playing guitars and stuff," giving the impression that the white students were not taking the protest seriously, "and we want you to leave."

By five thirty a.m. on April 24, Rudd, his fellow SDS members, and other white protesters had been kicked out of Hamilton Hall. They gathered up their clothes, food, and blankets. Some strapped on their guitars. As they left, an SAS freshman called after them in what sounded like a kind tone to Rudd, "Good luck to you, brothers. We're still together."

That night the SDS members felt tired and defeated. Some white protesters left, headed, no doubt, for the comfort and security of their beds. Rudd and his remaining white protesters headed back to Low Library. Three SDS protesters smashed a plank of wood through a door window and let themselves in. At President Kirk's office, a protester grabbed a wooden signpost that read "Office of the President of the University." Dozens of protesters streamed into the extravagant office, gawking at the Rembrandt painting, the Ming vases, and the enormous windows that looked out over Harlem, where nearly two-thirds of the residents earned less than a hundred dollars a week. Some protesters dug into Kirk's files, in search of paperwork about the university's connection with IDA. Others took turns sitting in his chair, sipping his sherry, and smoking his fancy cigars.

But New York City cops had gathered downstairs. Rudd and the other protesters couldn't decide what to do. Maybe they could barricade themselves in Kirk's office. Maybe they could hold a vigil in front of Hamilton Hall to stand in solidarity with the black protesters. They didn't have long to figure it out.

The police officers bolted up the stairs. About twenty-five protesters stood their ground. Rudd and dozens of others crawled outside through a back window. Soon after they escaped, the officers barged in. Administrators had called the police in to retrieve the painting and other valuables. But once inside, the head of the group of police declared that any students in Low Library would be considered "prisoners." The police made threats, but they didn't hurt anyone — this time. Some protesters wouldn't be so fortunate in the coming hours.

After a few hours of sleep in his apartment, Rudd returned to Low Library early the next morning, April 25.

He joined dozens of other white protesters who had escaped out the window the night before but then returned in the morning. The protesters who had stayed chastised Rudd for leaving. In a later meeting, Rudd and his fellow SDS members disagreed about next steps. Rudd resigned as chairman. He was just a member now — no longer in charge.

Inside Hamilton Hall, things were calm. Community supporters brought black protesters in Hamilton Hall food and medical supplies in case protesters got hurt. Black students treated their two hostages well; they didn't want to be charged with kidnapping. They asked Dean Coleman and Proctor Kahn if they wanted dinner. By late afternoon, SAS members released both hostages from Hamilton Hall.

On the rest of the campus, the demonstrations intensified. Protesters took over one building after another. By nightfall on April 24, protesters held five buildings. Black students and community supporters had barricaded Hamilton Hall. Two hundred students had occupied the president's office in Low Library. Allied groups had taken control of three other buildings.

By April 29, university administrators had had enough. They were getting pressure on all sides — from the faculty, from the protesters, and from the counterprotesters. They worried that violence might erupt. They sealed off the campus and ordered all buildings to be closed at six p.m. At one a.m. on April 30, the university called in the police. Provost Truman alerted his faculty that the New York Police were coming. The police department was ordered to remove all student protesters from campus buildings.

And the police did. Cops spilled out of police vans and buses and spread out across the campus. They wore helmets and carried billy clubs, ready to use whatever force they deemed to be necessary against the students.

Through an underground tunnel, police entered Hamilton Hall. SAS leaders instructed their group not to resist arrest. They knew how quickly police violence against black protesters could escalate. Police peacefully removed about eighty black protesters and led them to the police buses waiting outside. No one from the Hamilton building got hurt.

Elsewhere, chaos ensued. From the gates, Rudd could hear people screaming and crying. The cops forced their way past protesters standing guard around the other buildings. Police beat people who resisted.

They beat people who did not resist. They beat people who went limp and those who held up the two-finger peace sign. They beat protesters and counterdemonstrators alike. They dragged students down stairways. They pulled people by the hair, twisted their arms, and punched them in the face. They struck one professor in the head and did nothing to help as he walked away, bleeding. They beat medical volunteers. And they pulled handcuffed people into the police wagons that spread out over two blocks of Amsterdam Avenue.

By two thirty a.m., the police had arrested 720 people.

On campus, white protesters had experienced firsthand what black protesters had likely feared might happen. White students had not expected the degree of police aggression and violence. They were shocked at the police brutality.

Off campus, Rudd paced in front of a coffee shop across the street from the university's gates. The sounds of screams and sirens filled his ears. He picked up a brick from the ground and threw it at a post office window.

Wednesday, May 1. Rudd sat on a window ledge of Hamilton Hall. From his vantage point, he watched students spill across campus. Many of them had been arrested the night before. They were tired and disheveled.

But they were angry, too. Word got out that the New York City police commissioner had praised his police officers for handling "a potentially difficult situation without a single case of serious injury." And a front-page opinion newspaper article claimed, inaccurately, that students had vandalized Low Library. Most newspapers said little to nothing about the black protesters.

Rudd, still frustrated at being on the other side of the university gates the night before, was energized. "Strike! Strike! Strike!" he yelled.

Violence ensued once again. Uniformed cops rushed through

the crowd to join the group that was already at one of the campus gates. Cops brandished their weapons. They beat students with clubs. They kicked them. One student jumped from a window ledge onto a cop. Enraged to see their fallen fellow cop, plainclothes cops beat the student.

Rudd, desperate to stop the spiraling violence, climbed out onto a window grating. He screamed for everyone to stop. "The way to win is not to go out and fight the cops," he said.

The strikes continued. Columbia tried to reopen classes a week later, but most students refused to cross picket lines. The majority of classes were canceled. The university did not back down on approving amnesty. In late May, Rudd and four other protesters were suspended.

The university did back down on the gym construction. Columbia would never build Morningside Gym. For the time being, they would not encroach upon Harlem. Kirk resigned two months later. Protesters had brought about change.

For Mark Rudd and some of the white demonstrators, it was a catalytic time of their lives. That anger Rudd had felt at MLK's memorial was still churning inside him — and he still remembered the frustration he had felt when he was not on the other side of the school gates. He believed in MLK's civil disobedience but had adopted a more radical stance. He had witnessed police violence firsthand. The 120 charges of police brutality brought against the New York City Police Department were the greatest number of charges from any incident in the history of the department.

Later, when they felt the SDS was not doing enough, Rudd and some other SDS members formed a faction called the Revolutionary Youth Movement, then a radical, violence-oriented organization known as the Weathermen. Rudd remains an activist, passionate about making the world a better place, particularly for the poor and disenfranchised.

But it wasn't until a reunion at Columbia forty years later, when Hamilton Hall veterans pointed it out to him, that Rudd better understood the black students' perspectives — and what they had at stake. They recalled how the newspapers had focused primarily on the white protesters' actions — which not only distorted the truth but underscored the privilege and racism that the white protesters were trying to fight. Ironically, in a protest about racism, most journalists failed to report the black students' key contributions and their perspectives.

Cicero Wilson and many of the other black demonstrators had not attended MLK's memorial, but they knew his speeches, what he stood for, and what he had experienced. Even as they adopted King's approach of peaceful resistance, many still felt fearful. As one former student said, years later, "The worst racism I've seen is here at Morningside Heights" — adding that the only thing that kept him from leaving the school was the draft. For many of the black protesters, this was a scary time of their lives. The white students might have known about injustice and racism and wanted to end it; the black students had experienced it firsthand and needed to end it.

ROBERT F. KENNEDY

MARK KURLANSKY

y most enduring moment from 1968 took place on the living-room floor. I was a college student, and I had an apartment but it did not have much furniture. On that spring night, I was watching the California primary from Indianapolis, and because of the time difference, it was running late into the night, and I had gathered some pillows on the floor to watch the television and had fallen asleep. But I was confident. Bobby was going to win.

To me Bobby Kennedy was the solution to a problem I had been struggling with for a number of years, going all the way back to when his brother John was president and the name Vietnam, a place back then I had never heard of, started turning up in the news. I knew even then what it was going to become. My next-door neighbor, Richy, was sent over as an "advisor." Then every year more people that I knew and didn't were sent. The United States was using the technology of a modern super army to try to beat an impoverished people into submission. They were prepared to kill hundreds of thousands of them — millions, as it turned out.

When would it stop? How would it stop? It didn't look like the demonstrations I went to were going to stop it. Lyndon Johnson was never going to stop it, and Nixon wouldn't stop it, either. Eugene McCarthy would stop it, but he was never going to get elected.

Then came Bobby Kennedy. The solution. He could get elected, and he would stop it. I worked for him in the Indiana primary, which we won. I only saw him twice. Once by chance, sitting at the next table in the only reasonable restaurant Indianapolis had, Sam's Subway. He was eating ice cream, and years later I learned from his biographers that he loved ice cream — one of his boyish traits, like using the name Bobby.

The other time was in downtown Indianapolis, at a rally where he informed us that Martin Luther King had been murdered. News wasn't that fast in those days, and I hadn't known. I think most of the people in the crowd, in a black downtown neighborhood, were also hearing it for the first time. Later it was reported that he talked people out of rioting, pointing out that his brother had also been killed by a white man. But I don't think anyone was about to riot. The mood was not as much anger as sadness, a sadness that has never left me or probably most of the people there.

I woke up on the floor hearing the television talking about the Kennedy assassination. Why, I wondered, were they reviewing that now? But slowly I realized this was the next Kennedy assassination, the death of hope.

Nothing would stop the war now. In January 1971 it was still going on, and I was ordered to the train station in Hartford, Connecticut, where I was from, a blistered, weather-beaten wooden structure that had been built to ship troops to be slaughtered in the Union Army. We were sent to an induction center in New Haven, and most everybody had his own strategy about how to get out. I had no strategy, just this: I was not going to do it. After passing all the physical and psychological tests, we were lined up.

I walked up to someone in charge and said, "I think what you are doing is completely immoral, and I am not going to do it." The man looked bored. I think he was a sailor. He rolled his eyes and in a monotonous tone said, "Conscientious objector, line three." I had a hearing and an appeal and another appeal, and they kept turning me down, but I just kept saying that I would not do it. Finally they just let me go, and also they gave up on the war.

What I learned from the floor that June night in 1968 is that sometimes there are no strategies, nothing and no one to save you. If you are absolutely sure it is wrong, you simply have to say no. In the first student uprising in 1964, Mario Savio, a Berkeley student, said that sometimes "the machine becomes so odious, makes you so sick at heart, that you can't take part . . . and you've got to put your bodies upon the gears . . . and you've got to make it stop."

Now we have friendly relations with Vietnam, and it is a popular tourist destination. My daughter keeps saying, "Hey, Dad, can we go to Vietnam?" and I quietly rejoice that I never killed anyone there.

1968

July
August
September

NIGHTLY NEWS
Elizabeth Partridge

=== **SUMMER** ===

Hard to believe, Kennedy and King, both gone.

Now who will stand for us, say this war isn't right, stop this suffering and dying? Say things have to change, right here in our own country?

Big protests planned for Chicago at the Democratic National Convention next month. Who will the delegates pick for the next candidate now that we don't have Bobby Kennedy?

JULY 1968
American combat deaths: 813
South Vietnamese ally combat deaths: 1,409
Vietnamese enemy combat deaths: 9,632
Vietnamese civilian deaths: 376

I'm back in front of the television every night, watching coverage of the convention. There are more cameras outside on the protests than inside on the Democrats. Mayor of Chicago's throwing everything he's got at the protesters: cops, army soldiers, even the National Guard. Protesters have words, and fervor, up against guys with clubs, tear gas, revolvers, and rifles. Military police bring their jeeps, wrapped in barbed wire. Who do they think they're fighting?

Peace now, peace now, peace now, chant the protesters. Those two words, so simple, so clear.

Men in uniforms wade into crowds, cracking heads with their clubs, shoving people through plate-glass windows, lobbing tear gas canisters. Cop punches a news reporter right in the face, then arrests him.

Our own government, turned on us like mad dogs.

Protesters link arms, raise up their voices. *The whole world is watching. The whole world is watching.*

What good are words and fragile bodies against this madness?

When the convention's over, we've got Hubert Humphrey, vice president under Johnson, as the party's nominee. How can we trust him? Just going to take Johnson's policies with him right back into the White House.

AUGUST 1968
American combat deaths: 1,080
South Vietnamese ally combat deaths: 2,393
Vietnamese enemy combat deaths: 9,600
Vietnamese civilian deaths: 917

Some white boys at school wear dark-blue cotton workers' caps, made in China. Others wear Mao buttons, shiny red with a gold profile of Mao, like a coin. Everyone's equal under Communism, those boys say. It's a cultural revolution going on, making life better for the workers.

But Mao has locked China off from the rest of the world. A reporter says they're counting the dead bodies floating down the Yangtze River to the East China Sea. They're just guessing how rough things are going there by how many bodies are bobbing by on their way to a cold, wet grave.

SEPTEMBER 1968
American combat deaths: 1,053
South Vietnamese ally combat deaths: 2,164
Vietnamese enemy combat deaths: 39,867
Vietnamese civilian deaths: 443

PEOPLE, GET READY

Hippies, Yippies, Shoot-to-Kill Daley, and the Media

SUSAN CAMPBELL BARTOLETTI

Later, Abbie Hoffman would tell the story of his revolution this way: It was New Year's Day, and he and Jerry Rubin and three other friends were getting stoned in Hoffman's small ground-floor apartment on the Lower East Side of New York City. Outside, snow flurries floated over the street; inside, the loft apartment felt cozy and warm.

As Hoffman and his friends exhaled clouds of blue smoke and hallucinated bright swirling colors, they made protest plans for the coming year. Hoffman envisioned a movement of young people — hippies — with a shared political agenda: to protest the Vietnam War in a revolutionary way.

Someone shouted, "Yip!" and then Rubin shouted, "Pee! You need a little pee-pee in every movement." Abbie Hoffman doubled over in laughter. He rolled around the floor, laughing and cheering, "Yippee!"

And so, as Hoffman's retelling goes, the Yippie party was born in the early hours of New Year's Day, 1968. Over the coming days, the cheer "Yippee!" came to be spelled "Yippie" and the acronym YIP became the Youth International Party.

It's So Easy

Even when he wasn't high, Hoffman enjoyed a good joke. Jokes, said the psychologist Freud, can be a form of rebellion against authority, and Hoffman took great pleasure in rebelling against authority. Always had. His wild ways got him in trouble as a kid. The more his parents and other authority figures disciplined him, the more he acted up.

At thirty-one, Hoffman was older than the hippies he intended to rally. Like any effective political organizer, he studied their habits and their manner of dressing and talking and thinking. Wasn't there a way to bring together these disaffected, antiestablishment, counterculture young people?

To reach his target audience, Hoffman realized that he needed a different communication style, a way of speaking that would "let people experience feelings as well as thoughts" and "get people to act."

Knowing this, Hoffman developed his own "riffing" speaking style, one that appealed to emotions. Gone was the stuffy, formal rhetoric he'd learned in college. Gone were the reason and logic and facts used to influence audiences. Those were the devices of mainstream politicians—Republicans and Democrats—and the mainstream conservative culture that turned off the hip, now generation.

He also developed his own protest style: he turned to theatrical devices to garner attention, engage his audience, and cultivate a following, channeling the energy, playfulness, and bravado of young people. Yippies would rely on practical jokes, pranks, mockery, satire, gimmicks, stunts, and mythmaking in order to spread fear, create chaos and disruption, and shock and offend conservatives.

Even though Hoffman didn't trust the media, he studied the power it wielded over its audience and determined to use that power to his advantage. The entire nation would play—and be played—along on the streets, in newspapers, on the radio, and on national television.

"It's so easy," gushed Hoffman later. "All you need is a little nerve and a willingness to be considered an embarrassment."

A Festival of Life

In actuality, Hoffman's plan for a youthful revolution had begun months earlier, after his October 3 arrest for attempting to exorcise the Pentagon of its evil war-making spirits. (How else could the Vietnam War, napalm, and cluster bombs be explained, except as a creation of Lucifer? wrote Hoffman later in his autobiography.)

After levitating the Pentagon—you had to be there to "see" it, said Hoffman—he trained his sights on the Democratic National Convention, scheduled for Chicago during the last week of August.

The Yippies decried the Democratic convention as an "act of sado-masochistic folly" and a "Convention of Death." But, as Hoffman explained later, "Our battle in Chicago was not with the Democrats. Our battle was with those responsible for the Vietnam War."

To juxtapose the Democratic convention, the Yippies planned their own mock convention, one that would ridicule and villainize LBJ, his war policy, the electoral process, and the state of the union and exhort Americans to rethink the direction of their nation. They called the mock convention a "festival of life."

To spread the word, the Yippies produced a handbill with a decorative hippie graffiti–inspired banner that read "People, Get Ready!" The heading was a nod to a 1965 civil rights song whose lyrics called for people to rise above their differences and board a train for the promised land.

On Friday, March 22, Hoffman and other Yippies distributed the festival handbills at a massive midnight "Yip-in" at Grand Central Station in New York City. That night, an estimated three thousand hippies sang and danced under the station's vaulted ceiling to celebrate the spring equinox.

According to Hoffmann, the dancing ended abruptly when a young man climbed the information booth and yanked off the hands of a clock. The cops went "berserk," recalled Hoffman. "They began bashing heads without warning."

The brutality, Hoffman later wrote, "merely sharpened our determination."

Two weeks later, MLK was assassinated, and rioting broke out in 125 cities nationwide. The riots left thirty-nine people dead, more than 2,600 injured, 21,000 arrested, and incurred damages in excess of $65 million (about $433 million today).

Some of the worst rioting took place in Chicago, leaving nine black people dead, five hundred people injured, and twenty city blocks burned. The outraged Chicago mayor, Richard J. Daley, criticized the police for not handling the rioters and looters more forcefully. Taking matters into his own hands, Daley instructed the twelve thousand members of the Chicago police to "shoot to kill" any arsonist or anyone with a Molotov cocktail and "shoot to maim" any looters.

On April 11 President Johnson signed the Civil Rights Act of 1968. The bill addressed housing discrimination; however, it also included a rider that made it unlawful to cross state lines with the intention of inciting a riot. Those found guilty could face ten-year prison terms.

The law angered Hoffman, who argued that judges and juries would make examples out of protesters. "You measure a democracy by the freedom it gives its dissidents," he famously said, "not the freedom it gives its assimilated conformists."

Psychedelic Power

On March 31, President Johnson had announced that he wouldn't seek reelection. "Little did we realize that old warhorse LBJ would . . . quit," wrote Hoffman.

Johnson's withdrawal from the presidential race didn't dissuade the Yippies from their convention plans. Over the coming months, Hoffman worked day and night to organize the Festival of Life and spread the word, often getting by on three hours' sleep. "I was the 'itch,'" wrote Hoffman later, "the one who ran to the phone or into the street to make it happen."

A relentless Hoffman hounded Chicago city officials for parade permits and permission to sleep in Lincoln and Grant Parks, often granted to other organizations. He searched for housing, free food, and a place to set up headquarters near Lincoln Park.

The Yippies sought donations and raised money to print and distribute thousands of leaflets, political buttons, and posters. They wired daily messages to hundreds of underground newspapers.

Hoffman understood shock value. The Yippies made up their own news, fake story after fake story, and published the stories in widely circulated mimeographed leaflets and underground newspapers.

The stories targeted the fears, anxieties, and insecurities of city officials and convention-goers. One handbill announced that the Potheads' Benevolent Association had planted marijuana seeds in vacant lots throughout Chicago. "The long hot summer of 1968 is expected to produce ideal weather for marijuana growing," announced the handbill, "and most of the crop should be ready for smoking by the end of August."

Poking fun at conservative sexual mores, the handbill warned that "battalions of super-potent" Yippie men would seduce the wives of delegates and Yippie women would pose as hookers.

No delegate would be safe hailing a taxi: Yippies intended to paint ordinary cars taxi-cab yellow and ferry unsuspecting delegates out of state to Wisconsin.

Thinking of visiting Lake Michigan? Be prepared for the Vikings that would land their longboats on the shores, and ten thousand naked people floating in the water.

Don't flush the toilet. The Yippies threatened to burn the city down by pouring gasoline into the sewers.

Thirsty? Don't drink the city water. The Yippies planned to dump LSD into the reservoirs and send every resident on a "trip." Experts debunked the threat, assuring the panicked mayor that such a feat would require five tons of LSD, or 9 billion tabs, an impossibly expensive prank at roughly three dollars per tab in 1968 dollars. Still, Daley deployed the National Guard to protect the city water supply, an action for which he was later criticized.

Even LBJ's vice president, Hubert Humphrey, wasn't safe. Hoffman threatened to pull down the candidate's pants.

"There was no end to our plans," wrote a gleeful Hoffman. "Operating with a ridiculously small budget . . . we created a myth."

Hoffman's myth succeeded. Each threat, no matter how ridiculous, was reported to the police, who dutifully logged it and passed it on to crime-beat reporters, who often ran the stories alongside the more standard coverage of the convention and the Democratic candidates.

Later, Hoffman boasted about the free publicity. The more the Yippies pranced and pranked and acted ridiculous and made up news, the more the newspapers and radio and talk show hosts and the nightly news ate up the antics.

"We never had to pay for ads," Hoffman bragged. "The papers and the electronic media provided us with free coverage." Yippie organizers "stole" thousands upon thousands of dollars' worth of free publicity.

For Hoffman, the silly conspiracy theories and the buffoonery served a purpose. They helped to mobilize his young followers and get them involved. The rumors also spread fear, and in so doing, convinced mainstream politicians, the conservative culture, and ultimately the media of the Yippies' potential influence and power.

Be Sure to Wear Some Armor

Rumors and conspiracy theories serve a function for those who believe them. Such people often feel disaffected or alienated. No matter how much evidence or how many facts are presented to them, they believe false narratives because they don't like to be wrong and because the lies fit their own perspective of the world.

An infuriated Daley hated the idea that long-haired, make-love-not-war, peace-loving, do-your-own-thing, pot-smoking, acid-dropping, draft-card-burning hippies might make his Chicago look bad or rob the convention of its deserved media coverage.

Daley already had enough trouble on his hands: taxi-cab drivers, bus drivers, and even Illinois Bell telephone employees were threatening to strike during the convention week. The recent assassinations of MLK and RFK and the April riots were fresh on the mayor's mind.

The city seemed ripe for anything to happen. "The only thing that would surprise me is if nothing happens," a worried city official confessed to a *Time* correspondent.

Determined to protect the candidates, the delegates, and his city, Daley intended to squelch trouble before it started. He denied each Yippie request for a parade permit and permission to camp overnight in the parks.

Daley armed the entire Chicago police force with tear gas and riot gear, in addition to the standard firearms and clubs. Throughout June and July, the police practiced crowd and riot control. In 1968, police control tactics were simple: form a line, fire off tear gas, and charge into a crowd, swinging truncheons.

As the convention neared, Daley increased security: he canceled days off for the police department, ordering the entire police force to work twelve-hour shifts instead of the usual eight. Additionally, five thousand National Guardsmen and six thousand Army troops were placed on combat alert, ready with bazookas, rifles, and flame-throwers, if needed. An estimated one thousand FBI and CIA agents were assigned to roam the convention center and city streets and parks, some working undercover.

City workers sealed manholes around the convention site. The city issued warnings to reporters: avoid shooting photographs through upper-floor windows, so as not to be mistaken for a sniper. Merchants along the main routes and near the convention center were told to close windows. The police blocked city streets to all traffic except buses.

A witty *Time* magazine columnist advised delegates to pack "goggles (to protect the eyes from tear gas and Mace), cyclist's helmet (from billy clubs, bricks, etc.), flak jackets (from snipers), Vaseline (from Mace), Mace (from rioters), washcloth (from tear gas) . . . chrysanthemums (for flower power if cornered by militant hippies)."

An underground weekly newspaper, the *Chicago Seed,* warned demonstrators: "If you're coming to Chicago, be sure to wear some armor in your hair," referencing the 1967 Summer of Love pop song "San Francisco (Be Sure to Wear Flowers in Your Hair)."

On Monday, August 26, Daley would open the convention with a promise: "As long as I am mayor of this city, there's going to be law and order in Chicago."

Daley was determined to control public space and the media. So was Hoffman.

Yippie Leaks

A week before the convention opened, Abbie Hoffman landed at the Chicago airport wearing a T-shirt, cowboy boots, beads, and his usual crop of long springy hair. He still didn't have the parade permits or permission to sleep in Lincoln Park, but he was determined to get them.

In meetings, Hoffman purposely antagonized city officials, just as he had once antagonized his high-school teachers. He put his feet up on the table, leaned back in his chair, swore, and called officials by their first names. "Do you want thousands of people like me wandering through the streets of Chicago with no place to stay?" he asked. "You'll be creating a riot."

During a meeting with Deputy Mayor David Stahl, Hoffman lit up a joint. Stahl ordered him to stop smoking pot in his office. "I don't smoke pot," said Hoffman, straight-faced. "That's a myth."

Hoffman left the meeting empty-handed but soon hit upon a different tack. From an ABC reporter, he obtained a list of hotels, complete with hotel floor plans and room numbers where delegates were staying.

An underground newspaper printed the information with a blaring headline: "TOP-SECRET PLANS for LINCOLN PARK." The underground newspaper also advertised for "chicks who can type (and spell)" and "cats who have wheels." The program included a two-page manifesto, "Revolution towards a Free Society."

Rumors circulated about the Yippies, calling them "terrorists" who might "plant bombs." Restaurants profiled customers, refusing to serve anyone who looked like a protester. Building inspectors harassed landlords whose tenants offered housing to long-haired out-of-towners.

"The welcome mat was noticeably rolled up," wrote a delighted Hoffman. After that, he labeled all information "secret."

The Power of Om

On Friday, August 23, the Festival of Life opened with the nomination of a pig for president. At the Civic Center Plaza, Jerry Rubin introduced a hefty black-and-brown porker named Mr. Pigasus. "We want to give you a chance to talk to our candidate," Rubin told the crowd.

Several Yippies held signs reading "Pig Power" and "Live High on the Hog." The Yippies believed their candidate had much to offer the country. "If we can't have him in the White House," said a Yippie, "we can have him for breakfast."

The police squelched any hopes for the porky candidate. After a scuffle, the police arrested Rubin, Hoffman, several other Yippies, and the pig, charging them with public nuisance. The two-legged offenders were released, but Mr. Pigasus was hauled off to an animal shelter.

The next night, Saturday, the Yippies set a second pig loose in Lincoln Park. It was Mrs. Pigasus, the candidate's wife. As the police chased the pig, the Yippies shouted, "Pig! Pig!" Eventually an officer caught Mrs. Pigasus and tossed her into a police wagon. Mrs. Pigasus joined her husband at the animal shelter.

More theatrics and silly charades opened the festival. As the Yippies practiced the snake dance (supposedly a martial-arts technique for breaking through police lines), they charmed television and newspaper reporters who couldn't resist covering the looping and undulating protesters. The snake dance soon proved futile.

At the eleven p.m. curfew, the police lined up, wearing blue riot helmets and wielding nightsticks. Refusing to leave, demonstrators chanted, "Revolution now!" and "The park belongs to the people!"

The police readied to rush in, but the poet Allen Ginsberg stood among the protesters. Ginsberg closed his eyes, held out his hands, palms up, and chanted the sacred mantra "om."

The protesters joined in the chant. As the resounding "om" rose up, a calm settled over the protesters, and Ginsberg led them past the police and out of the park. It would be the last peaceful curfew.

"See You at Eleven O'Clock, Kid"

On Sunday, August 25, the city granted the Yippies permission to hold an afternoon rock concert. Throughout the morning, city park employees posted signs: "No sleeping in the park." An estimated five thousand attended the concert.

By the eleven p.m. curfew, about two thousand dwindlers left the park and congregated in the street. The police forcibly cleared the street, pushing, shoving, clubbing. The police targeted reporters, too, cudgeling them and smashing their cameras.

The next night, Monday, the protesters built flimsy barricades out of trash baskets and picnic tables. The police lined up three deep. This time television crews donned protective helmets and turned on their camera lights as police began to push the crowd. Protesters shouted "Pigs!" and "Oink-oink!"

Furious, the police lobbed tear gas canisters. The tear gas burned the demonstrators' eyes, blinding them temporarily and choking them.

The demonstrators fled to the street, but the police followed them, swinging their clubs, bashing heads. Again, the police turned on reporters and photographers, clubbing them to the ground and smashing their cameras.

Some of the police had removed their badges and nameplates. After leaving Lincoln Park, they roamed city streets for several blocks, attacking innocent bystanders, targeting those with long hair, and even pulling residents off porches and beating them in their own yards.

Then the police returned to Lincoln Park and slashed the tires of every car that bore a McCarthy campaign bumper sticker.

Later, the police would claim that the protesters had provoked them. Daley would excuse the police for attacking the reporters and cameramen and destroying their equipment, saying that the police were blinded by camera lights and unable to distinguish reporters from demonstrators.

Daley had never held a high opinion of reporters. The mayor often attacked the press for doing its job, later declaring, "A newspaper is the lowest thing there is."

To add insult to injury, when the reporters wrote about the police brutality, they found that higher-ups—editors or publishers following orders from city officials, perhaps — deleted the details from their articles.

The police acted strangely in other ways: At the south end of Lincoln Park, they lounged on folding lawn chairs, their riot gear alongside their chairs. Some officers pored over antiwar leaflets while others played a friendly game of catch with the hippies.

At the end of the day, the cops packed up their lawn chairs, collected their riot gear, and called out, "See you at eleven o'clock, kid."

And show up the police did. Throughout the week, they continued their clubbing rampage throughout the neighborhood.

The Battle of Michigan Avenue

On Wednesday morning, August 28, the last day of the convention, a tired and sore Abbie Hoffman ate breakfast in a restaurant. A police officer entered the restaurant and, spotting Hoffman, ordered him to remove his hat. Hoffman refused. The police officer left and then returned with six more cops. Four patrol cars and a police wagon waited outside.

Again, the cop ordered Hoffman to remove his hat. He complied, revealing a four-letter obscenity scrawled in lipstick on his forehead. "They dragged me right across the table, through the bacon and eggs, across the floor, then threw me against a squad car," said Hoffman.

The police held Hoffman for thirteen hours, moving him from precinct to precinct, cell to cell, treating him roughly. The police, Hoffman said, refused to disclose his location to his lawyers. By the time Hoffman appeared in court, he had missed the biggest clash of the convention: the Battle of Michigan Avenue.

At four p.m. on the last day of the convention, as Hoffman sat in police custody, an estimated fifteen thousand people rallied in Grant Park across the street from the Conrad Hilton Hotel. On rooftops, National

Guardsmen assumed positions. Below, blue-helmeted police in full riot gear surrounded the rally. Army troops and Secret Service were braced and ready.

Demonstrators sat in the closed-off street, holding transistor radios to their ears, listening eagerly to the convention's final events, hoping to hear that the delegates voted to adopt peace as a plank, or goal, in their party's platform. When they learned that the delegates had voted the peace plank down, shock rippled over the crowd. The shock turned to anger, despair, and a sense of hopelessness.

A young man raced to a flagpole. Grabbing the rope, he began to lower the American flag. Police pushed through the crowd to arrest him, but before they reached him, another group had lowered the flag and hoisted a red or possibly blood-splattered shirt in its place.

Police poured out of waiting buses and moved into platoon formation, jogging in place, their backs to the protesters. On command, the police pivoted and fired off tear gas. Seconds later, they rushed into the crowd, swinging clubs, cracking skulls and bones.

No one was safe. Not demonstrators. Not reporters. Not children. Not the elderly. Not bystanders and doctors who rushed to help those who had fallen, bruised and bloody.

Not those who fled on foot. The police chased them down the street and through a restaurant and into the Conrad Hilton lobby and continued their rampage. Panicked protesters pushed against a plate-glass window. The window broke, sending shards of glass everywhere.

The police had smashed the reporters' cameras, but security cameras mounted on the Conrad Hilton Hotel were recording the violence. For seventeen minutes the cameras rolled, silent witnesses. The cameras also caught something else: the demonstrators who didn't fight back, who realized the cameras were rolling, and who chanted: "The whole world is watching! The whole world is watching!"

Indeed, an estimated ninety million viewers watched the rampage on live television. Some watched in horror at the brutality; some watched believing the protesters had the beating coming; and some watched in fear that that their country was falling apart.

The police roamed city streets Thursday and into early Friday morning, again targeting young people with long hair. They stormed the fifteenth floor of the Conrad Hilton and burst into hotel rooms where young McCarthy campaign workers were sleeping. They dragged the workers from bed and beat them, too.

It seems a miracle that no one died during the rampage. In all, about six hundred protesters were arrested, the majority of whom were in their teens and twenties. Additionally, about a hundred protesters and 119 police officers suffered injuries, according to police reports.

Afterward, ten police officers were suspended for removing their badges and nameplates. Fourteen additional police officers received formal censure for their actions during the riot. Four officers were found guilty of using excessive force and recommended for dismissal.

Leave a Few Clues . . . and Vanish

The Yippies had begun as a joke, a joke that Hoffman took seriously. To him, revolution was "a game that's just more fun."

In 1968, Hoffman was a modern revolutionary, a provocateur determined to upend the political landscape. He recognized the power and potential of a captive television audience and understood how contagious the outrageous could be. "One of the worst mistakes any revolution can make is to become boring," wrote Hoffman about his exploits. Hoffman may have been many things, but he was never boring.

Later, Hoffman bragged that French philosophers had complimented him, telling him, "You came up with the idea that revolution could be fun. No one in history had thought of that, and only an American could have been so goddamned silly."

Was Hoffman's revolution simply fun and games? Did the Yippies' theatrics accomplish anything?

In early April 1968, LBJ withdrew from the presidential race. His vice president, Hubert Humphrey, won the Democratic nomination but ultimately lost to Republican Richard Nixon in the November election. In his autobiography, Hoffman admitted the Chicago protests had destroyed Humphrey's chances.

The Yippies never attracted a majority support. Their theatrics did not end the Vietnam War. The war continued for several more years, until the United States withdrew in 1973.

The Chicago Seven — Hoffman and six others — were arrested and accused of crossing state lines to incite the 1968 convention riots. Hoffman turned the trial into a circus, appearing in court stoned and once wearing a judge's black robe to court. When the judge ordered him to remove the robe, Hoffman did, revealing a Chicago police uniform underneath. The five-month trial ended in February 1970 with guilty verdicts for Hoffman and four others. In 1972, however, their convictions were overturned on appeal.

Abbie Hoffman rewrote the rules on protest. "Don't rely on words. . . . Rely on doing — go all the way all the time," he wrote. "Move fast. And once everyone is involved, shake it up, keep it fresh. . . . Get their attention, leave a few clues, and vanish."

Hoffman did vanish: to avoid drug charges for cocaine possession, he changed his name, and he and his wife went underground for six years. They emerged in 1980, and Hoffman served two years' prison time. That same year, Hoffman was diagnosed with bipolar disorder.

After his release in 1982, Hoffman continued his activism, writing and lecturing about environmental causes and the covert activities of the FBI and CIA in Nicaragua. In February 1988, Hoffman addressed Rutgers University students, telling them: "This is your movement. This is your opportunity. Be adventurists in the . . . sense of being bold and daring. Be opportunists and seize this opportunity, this moment in history, to go out and save our country. It's your turn now."

The next year, on April 12, 1989, Hoffman swallowed an estimated 150 tablets of the sedative phenobarbital and died, a tragic end for a man who seemed an indefatigable warrior for his convictions.

A fervent anticapitalist, Hoffman died nearly penniless, having given away nearly all the money he had earned from lectures and book sales. "He didn't die with a Rolex," said his brother Jack. "He died with a full heart."

Today, Hoffman's insights and instincts seem visionary. He understood how to manipulate the media, how to play to the fears of an audience, and how to use chaos and disruption to control and to rally.

What might Abbie Hoffman have accomplished in our current twenty-four-hour news cycle and with a social media account?

PRAGUE SPRING

MARK KURLANSKY

One of the greatest differences between the young people of 1968 and the older generations was the Cold War. After World War II, the Cold War divided the world into two camps: one controlled by the Soviet Union, the other by the United States and its allies. They faced each other with horrifying nuclear weapons. The college-age people of 1968 on both sides had grown up with the Cold War and the possibility of the world being destroyed by nuclear war at any moment. On both sides, they had spent their childhoods practicing for nuclear attack by hiding under their school desks. Most kids knew that a desk wouldn't save them and so were looking for ways out of this Cold War.

The nations of Eastern Europe had been taken by the Moscow-controlled Soviet Union in World War II. Russia established a network of Communist states loyal to Russia, either part of the Soviet Union or allied with and controlled by it. Communism was a political system with an ideology to end class difference, so there would be no rich and no poor, society would be free of material greed, and everyone would contribute what they could. But in reality it was also a police state, where no criticism was tolerated; the press, including radio and television, was controlled by the state and gave only the official message. People were not free to travel and foreign press was not allowed in, so there was little contact with the West.

The famous term "generation gap," invented in 1968 by the president of Columbia University to describe the huge difference between the young and older people in the United States, may have been even more true in the Communist Bloc. People born after World War II had a youthful enthusiasm for Communism and thought they could improve it. In Poland in 1968, students at the University of Warsaw protested a government decision to shut down a play. These were children of good Communists, and they thought protesting and demonstrating for the people's rights was what good Communists did. To their shock, they learned that they had no right to protest when they were violently attacked by police. The Communist ideology was of tremendous appeal, but the Soviet authoritarianism was not.

The brutal police-state tactics of the Soviet Union were maintained in other countries by the leadership in Moscow, who handpicked the leaders of the other countries. The only country where a leader rose to power from within the country's existing leadership was Czechoslovakia.

Czechoslovakia was the only country to legally vote in Communism after the war and was always Russia's most loyal ally. In the other countries, the Communist system was imposed by Soviet troops who invaded to drive out the Nazis. The troops were cheered as a liberating force in Czechoslovakia, and the Czechs tossed flowers at the liberating Soviet Army.

Some of the most important moments in history first pass unnoticed. Very early in 1968, a year packed with major news stories, perhaps the most important story of the year happened without a tremendous amount of attention. On January 5, 1968, Alexander Dubček was appointed head of the Czechoslovakian Communist Party. He was a dedicated Communist and a party insider. The only thing unusual about him was that he came from the minority Slovak part of the country instead of the dominant Czech part. They were two countries with different languages that had been put together by international treaty after World War I. Today they are again two separate nations.

Dubček was six foot four and usually described as gray, dispassionate, and difficult to understand. A boring speaker, he lacked anything close to charisma. His parents were Communists who had experienced repression years before the Communist takeover and moved to the Slovak community in Chicago. In 1921, when Dubček's mother was pregnant with him, they moved back. It was quipped that Dubček had almost been born an American.

From his youth, Dubček worked quietly for the Communist Party, never criticizing its incompetence, corruption, or brutality. He was a hardworking man who caused no trouble and worked his way to the top.

After taking power, Dubček explained, "The people were dissatisfied with the party leadership. We couldn't change the people, so we changed the leaders." Dubček took over for the unpopular strongman named Antonín Novotný, known as "Frozen Face," who'd held the title of president before him.

On January 5, the Czechs and the Slovaks cheered the appointment, but Dubček's wife and two sons cried. They seem to have been the only ones to understand that he had stepped into an impossible situation.

The people of Czechoslovakia believed Dubček was going to be better than Frozen Face. He was expected to reform Communism. Moscow believed they had placed a dedicated lifelong Communist as the new strongman. The people, especially the young people who wore blue jeans, grew their hair long, and listened to Western rock, were loyal Communists. They believed their new leader would make Communism better by making it more free. The expression for what they were seeking was "Communism with a human face."

The new leader of the Soviet Union, Leonid Brezhnev, did not share the same views. He had approved Dubček's appointment because Dubček was loyal.

In Czechoslovakia the people didn't see the possible rift between Moscow and their country. They had very friendly relations with Moscow, far better than other Soviet Bloc countries such as Poland and Hungary. The people began to stretch the rules, and their new leader said nothing. On January 27, three weeks after Dubček came to power, a newsstand opened in the center of Prague, the capital city, selling not only Czech and Slovak newspapers along with Russian and Polish papers, but also papers from the West: West German, French, and British news-papers. Never had this been allowed in the Soviet Bloc. The tall gray man said nothing.

Bit by bit, the local newspapers were changing, too. They exposed official corruption. They attacked and ridiculed the Soviet government. Newspapers competed with one another for readers by trying to find bigger and better scandals. It was revealed by the press that Novotný, who had never been under press scrutiny before, along with his son, had used a government import license to get the most luxurious Western cars, such as Alfa Romeos, Mercedes, and Jaguars, for the purpose of seducing women. Then the cars could be sold to the party elite for a huge profit and new ones obtained.

In March Novotný was forced to resign as president of the Communist Party of Czechoslovakia, in part because of the scandals in the press. Such a role for the press was unheard of in the Communist Bloc. Brezhnev and the other Soviet Bloc leaders made clear to Dubček that they were not pleased by his failure to rein in the press. But he was not sure how to do that. The press had taken off on their own and were out of his control.

The youth of Prague were enthralled by the possibilities a freer press offered them. The youth of the rest of the Soviet Bloc envied them. The youth of the West were fascinated by this freedom movement to the

east. Young people in Prague waved American flags, not to show support for America but to say they would not participate in the Cold War.
Westerners were not their enemies.

As spring approached, Czechoslovakia was becoming a more open
society one step at a time. Dubček complained that the people were
pushing too hard, going too fast. "Don't they realize how much harm
they are causing me?" he said to an associate in the Party. In each care-
fully worded speech, he always asserted his loyalty to the Soviet Union.

The people liked the gray man. They didn't mind his loyalty to
the Soviet Union. This was not a revolution, just a reform. They were
still good Communists. To replace Novotný, the gray man did not pick
the charismatic reformer that the enthusiastic people on the streets
of Prague wanted, for this would have outraged Brezhnev. He picked
an aging World War II hero who had fought with the Soviets. A huge
demonstration on the streets of Prague protested the decision. This in
itself was shocking. There were no demonstrations against government
decisions in the Soviet Bloc.

Today, what was called "the Prague Spring" is remembered as a
happy and exhilarating time. And in part it was. But in the month of
April alone, there was an average of one suicide of a government official per day. Government officials in the Soviet Bloc had never had to
cover up their misdeeds because the press had never examined them.
But now in Prague, newspapers and television were exposing officials
for crimes and corruption every day, and some of them could not face
this kind of exposure. Corrupt officials were interviewed on television, and viewers across the country could watch them squirm as they
attempted evasive answers.

If Dubček imagined—and many suspected he did—that he could
placate the public by giving them a small taste of democracy, he was
mistaken. The more freedom they got, the more they wanted. While
the young asked, How much can we get?, the tall and worried gray

Czech-born artist Peter Sís describes the experience of 1968 in his award-winning picture-book memoir *The Wall*. This image, originally created for the book, illustrates his feeling, after the arrival of the Soviet tanks, that a wall, briefly opened, was closing again and that the controlling masters would never let go.

leader asked how much Brezhnev would tolerate. Meanwhile the Prague Spring stretched into summer. As the weather warmed, Prague became the fashionable place for young people to travel, from not only the Soviet Bloc but the West as well.

For those warm and sunny months, the leafy streets of antique Prague were filled with young people from all over the world, and with music from the West as well as the new Czech rock. The Reduta, a small jazz club near the sprawling green lawns of Wenceslas Square, was always packed. Since only a little more than a hundred could fit in the club, the music and the young fans spread out to the square.

The Soviet Bloc had never seen anything like this. For the young people from both blocs on the streets of Prague, it felt like the end of the Cold War. In August, the *New York Times* headline read, "For Those Under 30, Prague Seems the Right Place to Be This Summer."

But on Tuesday, August 20, Anton Ťažký, an official of the Slovak Communist Party and an old friend of Dubček, was driving back from the countryside to the Slovak capital of Bratislava when he saw strange bright lights. Driving closer, he realized that they were headlights from tanks and other military vehicles with soldiers in foreign uniforms. He concluded that he must have stumbled onto the set of a movie. He went home and went to bed.

The tall gray man, still at work in a government session at eleven thirty at night, was informed: "The armies of . . . five countries have crossed the Republic's borders and are occupying us."

Russia invaded along with four loyal Soviet states — Poland, East Germany, Bulgaria, and Hungary. The four countries, under Soviet control, had little choice. The most reluctant of the invaders, János Kádár, the Hungarian leader, had tried to warn Dubček just two days before, saying that the Soviets were not the kind of people Dubček imagined and he did not understand with whom he was dealing. But Dubček prided himself on his understanding of the Russians and his lifelong friendship with them. Even his parents before him had been loyal supporters.

When Dubček learned of the invasion, tears slid down his cheeks. He said, "I have devoted my entire life to cooperation with the Soviet Union, and they have done this to me. It is my personal tragedy." He and the government refused to resign, declaring themselves to be the sole legitimate government of Czechoslovakia. They had the best-armed and best-trained army in the alliance, but Dubček ordered them not to resist. The country was invaded by four thousand tanks and 165,000 soldiers. Thirteen of the fifteen divisions were Russian.

For the most part, the invaders faced unarmed teenagers who tried to stop tanks by sitting in their paths. The tanks would not stop, and the protesters had to disperse. Some threw Molotov cocktails—the crudest weapon, a bottle stuffed with rocks and gasoline and a lit rag. Some did not know how to make them and just threw lit rags.

But mostly what the world saw and heard on radio and television was the great and powerful army that a generation ago had liberated Eastern Europe from the Nazis now marching against its own allies, against unarmed, nonviolent young Communists. Czechoslovakian television had managed to smuggle film of the invasion out of the country, and underground radio stations continued broadcasting from hidden locations.

It was the beginning of the end. The Soviet Union had lost its credibility. The governments of Yugoslavia and Romania, two nations of the Soviet alliance, denounced the invasion and permitted their citizenry to demonstrate on the streets. There were even seven protesters in the heart of Moscow, though they were quickly arrested. There were anti-Soviet demonstrations around the world, many of them by Communists.

In Czechoslovakia, young people were joining the Communist party at unprecedented rates in the hopes of taking it over. Dubček Clubs, with hundreds of members, were being formed around the country. When the Czech team did not perform well in the summer Olympics in Mexico City, the calm gray deposed leader sent the team a pointed message: "Don't hang your heads: What will not succeed today, may succeed tomorrow."

These were prophetic words from a man who was said to have been a boring speaker. It took twenty years, but in 1989, Communist rule and Soviet control ended in Czechoslovakia. By 1991, the Soviet Union itself dissolved. The last Soviet leader, Mikhail Gorbachev, said that their undoing all began in Czechoslovakia in 1968.

The Cold War had ended. Dubček never got his "Communism with a human face." He wrote that he came to realize that the Communist system was doomed by one central flaw: "It inhibited change."

The entire configuration of the world was now altered, and it had all started with this tall gray man in 1968. He remained popular and was often considered a candidate to lead the independent Slovakia, though in a typical Dubček complication, he had opposed Slovakia breaking away as its own republic. In 1992, at the age of seventy, he died from injuries caused by a car accident.

The great strength of his leadership was that in a time of violence all over the world, he always opposed violence or any kind of force. This gave both him and the people of Czechoslovakia a moral authority. In 1956, the Hungarians had staged an armed uprising against the Soviet Union, which was quickly defeated and had little impact. In 1990, Dubček said, "I think that in the long run our nonviolent approach . . . still has moral significance. In retrospect it could be said that the peaceful approach may have contributed to the breakup of the 'aggressive' bloc."

RUNNING WITH SHARP SHTICKS

Humor as a Force for Social Change

DAVID LUBAR

stick *n.* a piece of wood believed by parents to instantly pierce the eye of any child reckless enough to run while clutching it

shtick *n.* a bit of comedy; it can be sharp, dull, or blunt

The stand-up comic is the stealth assassin of the status quo. Audiences in the 1960s expected that the dramatic plays, movies, and television shows they watched would explore important contemporary issues. They expected comedies to make them laugh. And that is why humor is such a powerful weapon for delivering a message. If I see you marching toward me in enemy uniform, bearing a rifle and a malicious glare, I have time to seek shelter, or a bigger rifle. If you snap a pool cue over your knee (don't try this at home) and swing the fat end at me, I have a chance to duck. But if you dance up to me with a smile, tell me a joke, and then slice me from navel to chin with the stiletto concealed in your sleeve, I'm toast.

Before we look at the weapon, let's take a quick survey of the ammunition. Stand-up comedians rely on one-liners, stories, or a mix of both. The power of one-liners (which, despite the term, can consist of several lines) is that they require an intuitive leap from the listener, by means of leaving something unspoken, or, like haiku, they make an unexpected connection. This "aha!" moment creates a personal involvement for the audience. Essentially, the one-liner makes you think, whether you were planning to or not. The power of stories comes from empathy. Stories build bridges between people.

To get a feeling for the popularity of various types of spoken comedy in 1968, I looked at *Billboard* magazine's charts, which list the two hundred most popular record albums of each week. Music dominates the list. Comedy appears sporadically. (This doesn't mean comedy sales were poor. It just means significantly more people were willing to plunk down cash for the latest Beatles or Rolling Stones album than for the deadpan humor of a Bob Newhart or Shelley Berman.)

Let's take a look at the rankings before we consider the content. On January 6, 1968, the first comedy album on the list is Bill Cosby's *Revenge*, at #50. (In early 2018, Cosby was convicted on multiple counts of sexual assault.) He has several other albums on the charts that week. The next comedian we encounter is Flip Wilson, deep down at #194 with *Cowboys and Colored People*. Six months later, Cosby was at #16 with *To Russell, My Brother, Whom I Slept With*; Wilson had risen to #123; and Don Rickles appeared at #184 with *Hello Dummy!* In December, Cosby was #17 with *200 M.P.H.*, Wilson had fallen off the charts, and Rickles remained down at #184. (Arlo Guthrie's "Alice's Restaurant," which was recorded in 1967, appears on the charts throughout 1968. The humor-filled eighteen-minute hybrid of story and song, which chronicles his brushes with the law and the draft board, is a political statement against authority and the war in Vietnam. It doesn't fit into the stand-up topic, but let's give it a salute in passing.)

What were these comics saying? The content is telling. Bill Cosby sold well not just because he was funny but because he stuck with safe material. He talks about childhood experiences, parenting, and sports cars. It's uncontroversial fluff, a quiver of unsharpened shticks that, though masterfully constructed, present no threat to anyone. Ironically, by avoiding social issues, he actually brought about change by winning his way into many white households that might have never had a black visitor.

Flip Wilson's opening routine on *Cowboys and Colored People* describes his encounter with an Indian (as Native Americans were called back in the days of "Colored People") whom he tries to advise about overcoming discrimination. Viewed through the lens of twenty-first-century sensibilities and sensitivities, the routine, which draws laughs from references to peace pipes, feathered headdresses, wigwams, and buffalo nickels, might be seen as an example of racism, a brilliant parody of racism, or an uncomfortable mix of the two. But in a decade where Native Americans in "cowboys-and-Indians" movies were often played by white people with painted faces, most of Wilson's contemporary listeners would not find any irony in the routine, or in the next track, where he opens by stating that he hates midgets.

The album touches on various social issues, such as riots, but it does so gently, with no bite. Wilson talks about coming across a riot in Cleveland and deciding he needs to improve his appearance for the TV cameras covering the story. He gets a suit, in his words, "right out of the window." (Note that the laugh comes when the listener fills in the unstated information that the window was broken during the riots.) Wilson is, essentially, making fun of looting. It's political commentary in the lightest sense and, like Cosby's material, not threatening to the establishment. It doesn't speak at all to the rage and unrest that sparked the riot, or the need for change.

And then, after Cosby and Wilson, like a turd on top of a two-scoop ice-cream sundae, there's Don Rickles. I remember him from my youth. He was billed as an insult comic. We all laughed at his material on TV. He often visited our living room courtesy of Ed Sullivan and other variety-show hosts. But as I started to listen to *Hello Dummy!*, I was immediately struck by how blatantly racist and mean-spirited Rickles was. I have a high tolerance for edgy comedy. As a Jersey boy, I was raised to show affection by means of sarcasm. As a child of the '60s, I heard and told my share of offensive jokes when I was in middle school. Nevertheless, I couldn't listen to more than a minute of this abominable material. I thought about including an example, but I really can't present his words here, even in the interest of supporting my claim. It's that bad. And yet it was acceptable to a mainstream audience in 1968. Fortunately, there were people brave enough to speak out against this attitude of casual racism through their comedy.

Enter Dick Gregory, who was outspoken, political, brilliant, and bitingly hilarious. He was deeply concerned with civil rights, but he also took jabs at other contemporary social issues, including the Cold War and nuclear proliferation. Inspired by the activism of Martin Luther King Jr., Dick Gregory set aside comedy in 1968 to run for president. He returned to comedy the next year with a new album but remained very active in the fight for equality. While he could craft a killer one-liner, he also had amazing stories to tell. Which makes this a good time to look at the power of stories in comedy.

When Dick Gregory talks about buying a house in a rich white neighborhood while his neighbors are on vacation in Europe, we're drawn into his world. When he talks about shoveling snow and being mistaken, by a returning neighbor, for hired labor, we laugh with him and feel a bond. We're both on the same side of the joke, and it's the righteous side. We like to think we are better than the bigoted neighbor. And maybe the next time I see someone who is different from me in some way, instead of making assumptions, I'll remember the story of the snow shovel and not rely on stereotypes.

Note that a story can be personal and take the form of a real (or realistic) account, like Dick Gregory's tale of shoveling snow, or it can be more like a traditional joke, with exaggerated components, as in our next example, Moms Mabley's voting story.

Who?

Jackie "Moms" Mabley.

Who?

I should have mentioned her much earlier. The oversight was intentional, because it is a metaphor for her status in the history of comedy. If you ask people old enough to remember the 1960s, "Who paved the road for female stand-up comics?" most will say, "Phyllis Diller." And Diller definitely gets a lot of credit. In a male-dominated field, she became a star by making fun of herself. She used garish clothing, exaggerated makeup, and a wild hairstyle to diminish her attractiveness, and she used self-deprecating one-liners that focused on her appearance, such as, "My body is in such bad shape, I wear prescription underwear." (Note the unexpected connection her joke makes.)

But here's the thing. In many fields, there is a black person who achieved as much or more success, and broke more ground, than the familiar icon, but is not well remembered, or as well documented by history. In the case of comedy, that person is Moms Mabley, born in 1894 as Loretta Mary Aiken. Not only was she a popular performer on television in the 1960s, but she also produced a string of successful comedy albums, beginning with *The Funniest Woman Alive,* which achieved gold-record sales, and recorded a hit single version of the song "Abraham, Martin and John." And, unlike Phyllis Diller, she talked about race. Costumed like a cleaning lady, with a floppy hat, baggy housedress, and a noticeable shortage of teeth, she delivered her material with a distinctive, drawn-out style, and would unself-consciously chuckle at her own jokes. She had hilarious general material, such as when she describes an old man she married as "older than his birthday," but she also got political, and she often did so through stories.

When Moms Mabley talks about a black man in Selma, Alabama,

being given increasingly difficult and ridiculous tests before he can register to vote, including reciting the Bible backward and translating a Chinese newspaper, we feel, depending on our own experiences, either sympathy or empathy for those who face discrimination. The heavy exaggeration of this comedic tall tale is just as powerful a weapon as Dick Gregory's real-life anecdote.

Dick Gregory did appear on television, but mostly on late-night or afternoon talk shows. That's not where the big audience was. The big audiences were in prime time. So let's put away the dinner plates, gather in the living room, and turn on the television. The '60s were a great time for variety shows. And variety shows were a great venue for comedy. Keep in mind that in 1968 the typical television viewer had, at best, five or six stations available. Along with national networks ABC, CBS, and NBC, most cities had several local stations. Fewer stations meant more viewers per station.

And there were fewer other media available to siphon off the audience. There was no Internet. No streaming movies. No Roku channels. No Twitsnappintervinewhatever. Radio was fading as a major platform for comedy. On top of which, kids' lives weren't crammed with activities that ate up all their free time. The family got together each evening and watched network television. They were nearly a captive audience for any message, overt or subtle, that came their way.

But no matter how crucial your message, you couldn't get on television without the permission of the gatekeepers. And in 1968, the king of the gatekeepers, Ed Sullivan, was very conservative. *The Ed Sullivan Show,* which was broadcast from the eponymous Ed Sullivan Theater in Manhattan, had dress rehearsals on Sunday afternoons. Sullivan was known to edit comedy material before the evening's live performance, removing anything that might offend the conservative portion of his audience. (Since everyone watched Ed Sullivan, his audience spanned the political spectrum.)

While there was no way he'd allow his show to become a platform to fight for civil rights or against the war in Vietnam, at least
one subversive and progressive voice managed to slip in her political
agenda. Joan Rivers was solidly in the one-liner camp, but her material
set her apart, as did her appearance. She was well dressed in a simple
blouse and skirt or the classic little black dress, augmented with a small
broach or string of pearls, and didn't sport any exaggerated makeup or
teased hair. Her routine in the 1960s included shtick about how the
world treats single men differently from single women.

It was a bold move in a culture where nobody would blink at the
statement "A woman's place is in the home." Not Joan Rivers. Her place
was on the stage. As she recounted in an interview, early scouts for
The Tonight Show — a venue all comics aspired toward — felt she talked
about things women shouldn't discuss. She joked, for example, that her
seventy-seven-year-old spinster cousin met a ninety-two-year-old man,
and they got married because "they had to." (It should be noted that in
almost any arena, there is rarely one pioneer. Other comics had similar
messages, but Joan Rivers was the one who fought the hardest for the
spotlight and shined the brightest.)

So women and African Americans were speaking up, and Jewish
comics had been kvetching onstage for years. What about the rest
of America? As hard as I searched, I could find no evidence of Asian
Americans, Latinos, or other people of color performing stand-up
comedy on prime-time television or producing mass-market comedy
albums in the '60s, with the exception of Cuban American Desi Arnaz
(who was basically a straight man for his wife, Lucille Ball, on their
groundbreaking situation comedy, *I Love Lucy*), or Lebanese American
Danny Thomas, who was more a comic actor, in shows such as
Make Room for Daddy, than a comedian. (Comedian Bill Dana performed throughout the 1960s as the Hispanic character José Jiménez,
but Dana himself was of Hungarian descent.)

And while I would love to talk about the comedians who spoke out for gay rights, I can't. At a time when being openly gay could result in a jail sentence, a beating, or the loss of a job, there weren't any openly gay comics on network television. Unfortunately, a world that was barely able to accept that people were not defined by the color of their skin was nowhere close to ready to hear the LGBTQ message.

There were comedians who toyed with the boundaries. The very charming and snarky Paul Lynde, who sang, acted, and performed comedy, was able to wink at his sexual identity with jokes filled with innuendo, especially in his position on the game show *The Hollywood Squares*. (An example might get this book banned from school libraries, so I'll leave it to the reader to search him out. Hint: *innuendo* is a useful keyword.) Alan Sues, a regular on *Laugh-In*, played himself in broad strokes, with a bit more stereotypically gay affectations than Lynde. (Neither man openly spoke about his sexual orientation.) I suspected these comics gave young gay viewers welcome examples of people who didn't fit the straight, macho mold and yet were beloved performers on network television. Author and librarian Walter M. Mayes confirmed my reading: "Lynde and Sues were an example of coded, effeminate gays, typical of the period, and I adored them both, along with Charles Nelson Reilly."

Amid a sea of variety shows, which featured everything from plate spinners to ventriloquists to opera singers to roller-skating chimps, there arose a show that was pure comedy. *Rowan & Martin's Laugh-In* was a fast-paced hour of jokes, skits, bits, funny songs, and other shtick. If I were to base this essay solely on memory, I'd swear that the show was radical and biting in its political humor. I'd be wrong.

Upon viewing old episodes, I discovered that *Laugh-In*, for the most part, stuck with mocking safe targets like the Ku Klux Klan and openly racist presidential candidate Governor George Wallace. When they touched on more controversial subjects, such as school busing for integration, the joke was often devoid of all heat, as in, "I'm all for school busing. I've learned so much more in a school bus than I'll ever learn in a classroom." When a man, upon being asked what the country should do about the war in Vietnam, stutters and struggles to give a one-word reply of "de-escalate," Dan Rowan replies with the vapid and obvious comic rejoinder, "That's easy for you to say."

There was a reason for this lack of sharp social satire. In an interview, producer George Schlatter said he saw the show as a relief valve for a country stressed by things like an unwinnable war. He wanted to amuse both the left and the right. Like its audience, *Laugh-In*'s comedy spanned the political spectrum, but it rarely strayed from muted tones during the first season. In at least one area, *Laugh-In* reflected the darker side of its times. The writers were often guilty of objectifying or demeaning women. The show featured segments with bikini-clad women go-go dancing with random phrases and doodles scrawled on their bodies, and it had a running joke involving a woman getting punched in the face after saying "Sock it to me." (Presidential candidate Richard Nixon appeared on the show and spoke that phrase. He didn't get punched, but it's believed he got a bump in the polls.)

The other way in which *Laugh-In* was less effective at social commentary stemmed from its defining attribute — the rapid-fire delivery of the material. You never got time to think about what you heard. Before you could process a joke, or a funny piece of graffiti, three others had flitted past. Still, despite the barrage of sights and sounds, *Laugh-In* did acknowledge that the war was controversial and that bigotry existed. But in 1968, it failed to provide much food for the conscience or fuel for the resistance.

Bolder statements were needed. And they came to prime time because CBS decided to give a pair of comic musicians their own variety show, against show-killing ratings giant *Bonanza*, little knowing that those two jokers had huge social consciences. *The Smothers Brothers*

Comedy Hour premiered in 1967. The brothers had a likable routine. They'd start by playing an innocuous folk song such as "John Henry." At some point, guitarist Tom, who took the role of scatterbrain, would interrupt the music to say something silly. Dick, the straight man plucking the acoustic bass, would argue with him. Hilarity ensued. They'd finish the routine by completing the song.

But where Schlatter wanted a relief valve, the brothers, and especially Tom, wanted a pressure cooker. As the country descended into dissent and darkness spawned by an unwinnable war, riots, and a series of devastating assassinations, the brothers began to bring folk singers who'd written protest songs onto their show, most notably Pete Seeger, who sang the antiwar song "Waist Deep in the Big Muddy." They booked rock bands that appealed to a youthful audience. And they added young, hip comedians into the mix, like David Steinberg, Bob "Super Dave Osborne" Einstein, and Steve Martin.

George Carlin, who got very political later on, was a regular guest of the Smothers Brothers. His first performance on the show featured an innocuous-for-the-time routine called "The Indian Sergeant." In his autobiography, *Last Words,* he laments that "on the only comedy show that was actually taking a stand against the war" he didn't "sit down a month before and write something daring."

One of the early sketches involved "Goldie," a hippie played by improvisational comedian Leigh French. With the clever use of double entendres around words such as *high,* she was able to offer sly coded references to the counterculture without alerting the mainstream adult listeners, or the censors. (Though the censors had plenty of other issues with the show. They cut Pete Seeger's first performance of "Waist Deep in the Big Muddy" in 1967, but allowed him to return in early 1968 after a public outcry. Ironically, the first skit to be censored was one about censorship.) Buoyed by a writing staff of young rebels, including

Rob Reiner and Steve Martin, the show had so much appeal for young viewers that it gained impressive ratings.

The show offered another form of killer comedy: the satirical monologue presented in the form of an editorial or opinion piece. (It was once common for network executives, who tended to be very conservative, to go on the air to give an opinion about a topic in the news. It was usually something pedestrian in nature, like a highway project.) Pat Paulsen was the master of editorials, delivering lines with deadpan humor. His material was wonderfully subtle. For example, "But we are not against censorship, because we realize there is always the danger of something being said." He ran for president several times, as an extended form of comedic performance art, using campaign speeches as a platform for his humor.

The war and censorship were frequent targets on the show. But the battle with the censors grew more heated as the brothers got more daring. Tom Smothers admits losing his balance as a comedian when he started talking directly to the studio audience to fill in for the censored segments. In the end, the program was canceled because the brothers refused to show each episode to the network ahead of airtime, as required by their contract. In deciding a later lawsuit, the court ruled that CBS had violated the contract, but the show was long gone by then.

Harry Belafonte, who got cut from the season-three opener for singing "Don't Stop the Carnival" in front of news footage showing violence at the Democratic convention, later summed up the power of the show and the danger of censorship in an interview, saying, "No matter what one may have thought about some of the ideas expressed, the truth is that, by and large, they got expressed. And when that was violated, it really had enormous significance."

Like Carlin, other comedians, including the legendary Richard

Pryor, made pivotal swings from comfortable comedy to biting commentary toward the end of the decade. As much as comedy helped change the world, the world inspired comedy to change.

There are so many worthy and trailblazing comics left unmentioned, including Lenny Bruce (who died in 1966), Mort Sahl, Godfrey Cambridge, and satirical songwriter Tom Lehrer, who, while not a stand-up comic, was a crucial voice of the 1960s. But I'm already in danger of running long, which is great in football but not appreciated in the book world. So let's sum up, wrap up, and move on. There's often no way to know whether a joke or a story brought about any change. But the Vietnam War did come to an end, the threat of nuclear destruction ebbed, young people got involved in politics, and minorities made progress against discrimination. On top of which, we now can see comedians like Gabriel Iglesias, Margaret Cho, Aziz Ansari, and Julia Scotti in prime time.

There is no way to guess how many hearts were swayed. But as I look into my own heart, and the changes it's experienced across the decades, from the little kid who swapped Polish and Italian jokes with his classmate to the writer who strives to keep diversity in mind and a social conscience on his pages, I know that the comedy I grew up with, and the current comedy it spawned, has made a difference to me. I don't think I'm alone.

October
November
December

1968

NIGHTLY NEWS
Elizabeth Partridge

===== FALL =====

Two American sprinters, Tommie Smith and John Carlos, win first and third in the 200-meters at the Mexico City Olympics. Smith breaks the world record, coming in at 19.83 seconds.

They're standing proud on the podium. Proud of winning, proud of being American, proud of being black.

Our national anthem comes over the loudspeakers, and they each raise a fist into the air, clenched tight in the Black Power salute. Same time, they look down at the ground. Stay just like that till "Stars and Stripes" fades away.

Stadium falls silent.

Seems like next the whole world goes crazy. Angry people saying the American flag and anthem have been desecrated. Not supposed to mix sports and politics.

Smith and Carlos expelled right away from the Games and sent home. Fired from their jobs.

They're from my state, California, only a few miles away from where I live. It hits me hard. There sure are plenty of ways to cut people down without using clubs and guns.

OCTOBER 1968
American combat deaths: 600
South Vietnamese ally combat deaths: 1,169
Vietnamese enemy combat deaths: 12,215
Vietnamese civilian deaths: 440

Tuesday, November 5. Watching the election returns, want to see who'll be our next president. Humphrey's up against Richard Nixon, the Republican Party nominee. Nixon's all for law and order, says we've slid into permissiveness.

Six o'clock news, race is close. Eleven o'clock news, still too close to call. Next day, we hear Nixon won. He's for the non-shouters and the non-demonstrators, pledges to bring order to the United States.

My grandfather says that for the first time since he turned twenty-one he didn't vote for president. He's a lifelong Republican, colonel in the U.S. Army. Says he couldn't vote for *that man,* left the box blank.

My Democratic mother just shakes her head. Doesn't like to think we've got a president even her dad wouldn't vote for.

NOVEMBER 1968
American combat deaths: 703
South Vietnamese ally combat deaths: 1,408
Vietnamese enemy combat deaths: 10,319
Vietnamese civilian deaths: 355

Christmas Eve. Anybody with a TV is watching tonight. Three astronauts circling the moon in a space capsule, Apollo 8, sending live footage of the moon's crater-pocked surface. Turn their camera back toward us, so we see what they see. Earth so far away, it's just a tiny cloud-swirled marble in the vast blackness of infinite space.

Can't imagine those astronauts can even pick out Vietnam, a tiny sliver of land tucked under China, laced with clouds. I know they can't see how we're tearing each other up around here.

The astronauts take turns, read to us from the book of Genesis. Their voices are roughed by static, but full of wonder: *In the beginning . . .*

DECEMBER 1968
American combat deaths: 749
South Vietnamese ally combat deaths: 1,509
Vietnamese enemy combat deaths: 15,478
Vietnamese civilian deaths: 5,389

STUDENT SACRIFICES

Massacre at the Plaza de las Tres Culturas

OMAR FIGUERAS

I.

Throughout Mexico City, yellow, blue, and pink banners fluttered high above the streets. "Everything Is Possible in Peace," crowed billboards. The capital city of Mexico awaited its athletes. For the first time, a Latin American country would host the Olympics, and the city was dressed for the occasion. From the banners to the billboards to the hostesses in their pantsuits and miniskirt uniforms, all were emblazoned with the logo MEXICO68. With the eyes of the world upon it, the Mexican government was determined to show that its country was as modern and progressive as any other industrialized nation on the planet.

But nothing was peaceful in Mexico City. Although he had previously been able to tamp down protests in his country, President Gustavo Díaz Ordaz could not contain the growing unrest of the nation's youth. He feared students would take their French, Czech, and American counterparts' protests as an example and use the looming international event as a platform to embarrass Mexico, and, more important, himself. His Mexico had always been capable of effectively quashing dissent in any of its forms; the opposition was usually bought off, and if they held to their convictions, they were killed. The governing elite was determined not to be humiliated in the eyes of the world by a group of college kids. The trouble began in July.

Teams from two rival high schools were finishing a soccer match the afternoon of July 22, 1968. A fight erupted as the players left the field. Students from Vocational Schools 2 and 5 at the National Polytechnic Institute and those from Isaac Ochoterna Preparatory shouted, pushed, shoved, perhaps punched and kicked one another. Soon the scuffle erupted into the streets and caught the attention of the local gangs of the neighborhood, the Cuidadelans and the Spiders.

Violence escalated throughout the Polytechnic, spilling into the Plaza de la Ciudadela and the surrounding neighborhoods near the historic center of the ancient city. Residents called police.

Swamped by the teens, the police summoned the *granaderos*, the ruthless government riot squads trained to suppress such incidents. Clad in protective gear, some holding clubs and others rifles, the officers responded brutally. The riot police descended into the crowd, where they cracked bones, broke skulls, and fired tear-gas grenades.

Skirmishes continued over the week, and on July 28, Poly students once again engaged the *granaderos*. Overwhelmed, the youths fled to their campus on foot, but the *granaderos* followed. Fearing for their lives, the students locked the doors inside one of the buildings and barricaded themselves. Students fashioned weapons from what furniture they found in the college offices and prepared to defend themselves. They had no water or food, but driven by their passion, they held their own.

Two days later, on July 30, bazookas blasted open the front doors and in poured the troops. The *granaderos* apprehended everyone inside and indiscriminately beat the students. All were jailed; most were tortured.

Angered by the government's brutality, students from all over Mexico united in a common cause: If their government could over-react when breaking up a post-soccer-game scuffle with such brutal force, what else were they capable of doing to their people, and especially to their youth?

This was not the first time the *granaderos* had overstepped their bounds, and for years people had demanded that they be abolished. Teachers marched in 1958, and railway and factory workers rallied in 1959, complaining of low wages and inadequate housing. They were met with lopsided force, jailing, and torture. The government was accustomed to showing merciless aggression toward its people. This disrespect and intimidation is what ignited the students' rage and birthed their movement.

Yet it is also true that the government had provided decades of middle-class stability and development. The Mexican government offered its people a devil's bargain: it could provide stability by brutally silencing dissent. Until now, most Mexicans had accepted the trade-off. It was this track record that allowed the government to sell the Olympics as the crowning glory of the "Mexican Miracle." With student protests brewing, the Olympics would be the test: Could the government keep order? And at what price?

II.

Over the summer, students formed unions, and groups spread throughout many of the college campuses. The students suspected that their groups had been infiltrated since they were funded by the Partido Revolucionario Institucional (PRI), founded in 1929. The PRI was the predominant Mexican political party, and the only party that had held power since its birth.

Imagine if only one political party ran the country, and every student meeting you attended, every group function and event you were a part of, was colored by that ruling party. Students deemed these PRI-backed organizations "mummies," embalmed creations of an old, out-of-touch, and repressive government. Now imagine that all the information shared in those groups was slanted toward this mummified party's agenda. The members of these groups also acted as watchdogs for the PRI and reported which students even hinted at the least bit of rebellion. No one could speak freely or voice unfavorable opinions about the government, in or out of the classroom. PRI spies infiltrated all student groups and organizations, and secret records were kept of who spoke favorably of the Communists and who criticized Díaz Ordaz. Students turned in other students.

On August 8, students from seventy college and preparatory schools gathered and formed an alliance, the Consejo Nacional de Huelga (CNH), or National Strike Council. The CNH would be the students' united voice, expressing their demands and organizing the protests and marches.

All throughout that August, CNH members handed out leaflets on buses and trolleys, in food markets and big department stores, telling of their upcoming events. Members held "lightning meetings" on street corners, scattering at the hint of an approaching policeman or *granadero*. Word of the CNH's intentions quickly spread through this guerrilla marketing campaign, and railway and factory workers joined the movement. Having seen the escalation of the fighting on television or firsthand, some older Mexicans sympathized with the students.

It was dangerous. Student Carlos Galvan recalled soldiers arresting him and his friends. "They made us line up with our hands up, and took the ones with long hair," said Galvan. "They made one kid kneel down and lopped his hair off with a bayonet . . . Then they told us to line up with the rest of the kids. 'Here's a little farewell present for you.'" Using their rifle butts, he recalls the soldiers "started hitting us as though they were breaking piñatas."

At first, the CNH expected crowds of five thousand or so. But when the numbers began to climb, and ten thousand, fifty thousand, one hundred thousand people came out in support, the government could not turn a blind eye.

On August 23, an estimated three hundred thousand individuals—

college and high-school students, workers and professionals, parents with their children—demonstrated through the streets. The crowds marched to the central plaza and beating heart of the capital, the Zócalo. Protesters spent the night underneath the presidential balcony in hopes that their demands would be addressed: freedom for all political prisoners, disbanding the *granaderos,* and repeal of laws sanctioning imprisonment of those who gathered in groups of three or more people.

Sunrise came, and the bleary-eyed crowd disbursed peacefully but sadly, as there was no response from the president. In fact, the nonviolent protest angered him, and the government began to escalate its retaliation. On September 1, during his annual delivery of the Informe, the nationally televised state-of-the-union address, Díaz Ordaz said:

> "We have been so tolerant that we have been criticized for our excessive leniency, but there's a limit to everything, and irremediable violations of law and order that have occurred recently before the very eyes of the entire nation cannot be allowed to continue."

Newspapers refused to print anything critical of the government or the PRI, so subversive information had to be shared in more creative ways. The CNH gathered again, this time at the Plaza de las Tres Culturas on September 7. Students tied signs to dogs and set them loose throughout the city; others from the Poly inflated balloons that popped once they reached a certain height, releasing CNH propaganda. They scattered flyers throughout the neighborhoods that read "Freedom for Political Prisoners" and "Death to Cueto," the Mexico City chief of police. Slogans were painted on fences; police would cover the lettering with gray paint, and just as fast, the students would paint over the gray paint. If caught in the act, perpetrators were shot on sight.

Police apprehended students, professors, and delegates all throughout September; officers detained them in their offices, factories, schools,
or homes—tying their hands behind their backs and draping burlap
sacks over their heads, the coarse fabric loose enough to allow light in
but dense enough that it was impossible to see through.

Félix Sánchez Hernández, a worker at the Sanborn chocolate factory, recounts the day of his arrest (October 1, 1968): "Four men
dressed in civvies entered the factory with pistols in their hands and
immediately started roughing me up. They grabbed me and hauled me
out of the building."

Despite these arrests, students continued to show up at the marches
in record numbers, and the people continued to support them. Crowds
of a quarter million to three hundred thousand flooded the Zócalo and
they chanted for reform. A river of people engulfed the base of the Angel
of Independence monument, circling its tower and bursting through
the neighborhoods like living plasma, pumping through the deadened
veins and arteries of streets, reviving the city and all of Mexico.

Not everyone agreed with the student movement. Some saw the
students as ungrateful, naive, and selfish. Although most Mexicans
cared about the condition of the workers and the country itself, some
viewed the college students as spoiled ideologues who were out of touch
with their reality.

"I'm a mother of a family and I was simply dumbfounded by the
attitudes of the university professors," said María Fernanda Vértiz de
Lafragua, a grade-school teacher. "They were as bad as the kids: they
seem to delight in stirring up trouble."

Many workers saw the students as privileged middle-class whiners
and accused the CNH of being meddling visitors who did not understand their lives. The workers felt they were stuck in ways of living
and working that they could neither improve nor escape; the protesters
were merely intrusive, unwelcome troublemakers.

Some questioned whether they were legitimate students. "Who did those kids think they were anyway?" said Yolanda Carreño Santillán, a cashier at El Fénix Pharmacy. "The first thing I'd ask them would be to show their semester grades."

There was a growing split between students who were in touch with ideas from around the world and both their government and the working class. The families of the soldiers employed to put down the movement were bitter toward the students. Fathers, who were often the sole breadwinners of their households, had been recruited and spirited away from their families for weeks. This was a conflict of culture as well as of income. "It's the miniskirt that's to blame," said Leopoldo García Trejo, a postal worker. Perhaps the rising hemline was the barometer of the time, indicating a rise in liberal thought and climbing blood pressures.

As the country splintered into opposing camps, protests continued and grew more heated. The government dressed some of its special forces as students, ordering them to turn buses over, set fires, and assault women, all in an attempt to discredit the CNH.

In turn, though, some believed that students were provoking the police. But who you blamed for the growing unrest depended on what you believed — and what you had witnessed. Marcos Valadez Capistrán, a civil engineering professor, witnessed violence from the police. "A child or a teenager who badly misbehaves rightly deserves to be reprimanded," said Capistrán, "and even punished severely, but even so you shouldn't bash in your ten-year-old son's head with a chair or beat him to death simply because the kid has given you a kick in the pants in a fit of anger or hysteria."

Children joined in the campaigning, taking broomsticks and wooden rifles and marching in and around the *granaderos* and soldiers. Each group agitated the other, tensions rose, and the situation quickly spiraled out of control.

III.

It drizzled during the early evening of Wednesday, October 2, two weeks before the Olympic Games opening ceremonies. The CNH's event was set to start a little after five that afternoon, but things were running late. Once again, approximately five thousand people gathered at the Plaza de las Tres Culturas near the Chihuahua Building, most amassing underneath a third-floor balcony where student speakers addressed the gathering crowd. One of the oldest parts of the city, the plaza encompasses three cultures because it features ancient Aztec ruins, a Spanish colonial cathedral, and modern office and housing complexes. It both honors Mexico's past and displays its vibrant present.

Students ran a massive leaflet campaign for this demonstration, and, having witnessed the summer protests, many residents of the Tlatelolco district and members of the workers' unions turned out to support the event.

John Rodda, a sports reporter for the British newspaper the *Guardian,* who was in Mexico City to cover the Olympics, walked to Tlatelolco to see the demonstration. Like many others, he was drawn to the plaza out of curiosity. With his press pass in hand, and armed with very little Spanish, Rodda edged his way to the space below the balcony through the crowd of young men and women in their late teens and early twenties. The blades of two military helicopters whipped overhead.

A student standing near Rodda commented, "'One from the police, one from the military.'" Then two green flares shot up from behind the church. "There was a buzz in the crowd," Rodda wrote. Soldiers and police units were spread throughout the square, rifles fixed with bayonets and loaded machine guns.

The CNH considered calling off the protest. The speakers were preparing to disband for the evening when one of the helicopters released a greenish-blue flare. Someone—a sniper, declassified government documents would later prove—stationed in a building near

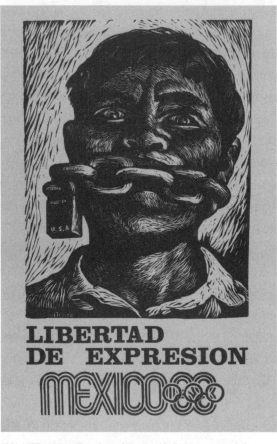

This 1968 poster, "Freedom of Expression," shows support for the student protests that took place before the Olympic games in Mexico City.

the gathering fired his gun. Tanks rolled into the plaza. Two flanks of soldiers approached from opposite ends, sealing off the exits for the unarmed crowd.

Shots rang from one of the adjacent buildings. People screamed and began to run. More rounds echoed as the army, police, and *granaderos* continued to fire on the crowd. First one student, and then another, and then another fell. Others hit the ground and then scrambled to their feet. They were followed by the sounds of tanks, rifles, machine guns, helicopters circling above, and more sniper fire pinging off the stone walls and floors.

The ancient church of Santiago Tlatelolco locked its doors once the shooting started and kept them shut; the dead and wounded were left to bleed on the cobblestones. The sun set, and darkness engulfed the plaza, which echoed the screams and groaning of the injured.

"The worst moment came when someone with a machine gun high up was spraying bullets down," Rodda wrote, "and the firing line was catching the edge of the walls and sending up sparks and sprinkling the corner where I was covered in cement and concrete chips. A girl student wearing slacks was hurt, but whether she got a direct hit or was caught from a ricochet I cannot say."

Rodda observed men who were not crouching or avoiding the gunfire. They walked through the plaza dressed in plain clothes and wore a single white glove or handkerchief wrapped around their left hand. These men — later revealed as the Olimpia Battalion, a secret security detail created specifically for the Games — moved undisturbed to and fro after the shooting started, and the army and police did nothing to stop them.

Discarded shoes and bags were sprinkled like offerings to the dead. No one was spared. The lifeless bodies of children, pregnant women, and Red Cross and railway workers were spread throughout the plaza. Among the dead, recognizable only because of the distinct geometric pattern of the lines on her uniform, was one of the Olympic event hostesses wearing her miniskirt.

In 2000, for the first time since its creation, the PRI lost its hold on power. In 2003, President Vicente Fox declassified government documents and records that revealed that the snipers who had started the shooting were members of the presidential guard, who had been ordered by Díaz Ordaz to provoke the army. Entrenched in the neighborhood's buildings, they fired on the troops, who, in turn, fired on the students.

The death toll has never been firmly established. Some government reports say thirty; others say three hundred. Rodda estimated the dead as near five hundred, but neither this nor any figure can be verified. Hours after the bloodshed, trucks were brought in and the dead were hauled away. Teams of maintenance workers scrubbed the stones and pavement, leaving no trace of blood. There was scant mention of the events the next day in the local newspapers.

Ten days later, amid some apprehension that the violence would resurge, Mexican hurdler Enriqueta Basilio made her way into the Estadio Olímpico Universitario and became the first woman to light the Olympic cauldron, and the Games went on as scheduled.

Many other students were arrested in the weeks and months that followed October 2. Some were tried under trumped-up charges and incarcerated for months, if not years. By the end of 1968, the CNH was dissolved. Although the raging fire of protest was smothered and none of their demands were met, the embers of the students' passion smoldered. The uprising signified to Mexico how the youth of a nation could challenge the status quo, bring those in power to task, and provide hope for improvement.

Fifty years on, Mexico honors those who died on October 2 and condemns the government for their heinous actions. However, after regaining control in recent elections, the PRI has once again suppressed access to information dealing with the October 2 massacre. Widespread political corruption, violation of human rights, and lack of security still plague Mexico. Despite hardline rule and oppression, like the flame brought to the New World from ancient Greece, Mexico's citizens' desire for economic and social stability, democracy, and representation burns eternal.

RUNNING INTO HISTORY

Mexico City Olympics

JIM MURPHY

The excited murmurs of the spectators began turning to cheers the moment the eight finalists for the 1968 men's Olympic 200-meter race began emerging from the stadium tunnel. The shouts, applause, whistles, clapping, and the clicks of thousands upon thousands of cameras intensified as the men came into full view, the sound rippling like a giant wave until all eighty-three thousand people in Mexico's Estadio Olímpico Universitario rose to their feet to welcome the athletes.

It was a genuine, enthusiastic greeting, but it was also something much more—a call of expectation, even a demand. The 1968 Olympics produced an unbelievable number of Olympic and world records in all events. Competitors in men's track and field alone would eventually set ten Olympic records and nine world records. These would include Jim Hines becoming the first human to run 100 meters in under ten seconds (9.95) and Bob Beamon's astonishing long jump (8.90 meters, or 29 feet 2½ inches) that beat the existing record by almost 22 inches. The crowd was hungry for another record.

All these men were elite, world-class athletes. They knew what everyone watching was hoping for; they knew that spectators expected a running performance to remember for the rest of their lives. But they also knew that to run well, to have a chance of becoming a part of Olympic history, they had to focus their every thought on the race ahead.

Most of these men had other, weightier distractions to shrug off for the time it would take to run 200 meters. The United States athletes had experienced a year of national turmoil and violence. The eleven-year-old Vietnam War had already resulted in the deaths of over twenty thousand U.S. soldiers; 1968 would almost double the total, with nearly seventeen thousand more soldiers killed.

In April, Martin Luther King Jr., leader of the civil rights movement for racial equality, had been assassinated, followed in June by the killing of presidential hopeful Robert F. Kennedy. Riots followed in over 120 cities that resulted in death, injuries, and destruction.

Many of the Olympic athletes were so upset by this avalanche of harrowing, tragic events that they suggested the Games be called off or at least postponed. Going ahead with sporting events seemed inappropriate, even trivial, considering what was taking place in the world.

This feeling intensified and spread throughout the more than a thousand Olympic athletes just ten days before the official start of the Games. That was when ten thousand students and civilians assembled in the Plaza de las Tres Culturas in Mexico City to protest harsh and unfair government policies. Sometime after 6:15 p.m., government troops opened fire on the crowd, killing anywhere from forty-five to three hundred people. Soon the call of the athletes to end the Games was echoed by an international chorus of politicians and sporting organizations.

Avery Brundage was the head of the International Olympic Committee (IOC) at the time. When he got word of the protest, he went into action.

Brundage was an ardent defender of the Olympics and didn't suffer fools (which included anyone who disagreed with him). His autocratic style had shaped the Olympics into a powerful and financially

successful sports machine. He was also ferociously opposed to any boy-
cotts of the Games. Back in 1936, for instance, when he was the head
of the U.S. Olympic Committee, there had been calls for the United
States to boycott the Summer Olympics in Berlin, Germany. In power
four years, Adolf Hitler's government had already passed over 430 anti-
Jewish laws. But when Jewish organizations in the United States voiced
opposition to the Games, Brundage dismissed their concerns. Even
when German politicians and athletes at the Olympics raised their
hands in the Nazi salute, Brundage brushed it aside as unimportant.

Brundage did much the same in 1968. To cancel or even postpone
the games, he argued, would cause financial harm to Mexico and further tarnish its national image. In addition, he pointed out that the
athletes had spent years training for this chance to be a part of Olympic
history; why throw it away now? In the end, the athletes backed down
and the Games went on.

The finalists for the 200-meter race walked over to the aluminum
starting blocks, shaking their legs to keep them loose, relaxed. The
world's turmoil and the brush-off by Brundage were in the past, at
least for the time being. Each wanted to concentrate his every ounce of
energy into a sudden burst of speed.

After taking their sweat suits off and checking the laces of their
spikes, they approached the line when the starter judge commanded,
"On your marks." The vast crowd quieted in an instant, tense, waiting,
hoping.

Slowly, carefully, the runners eased themselves into their blocks.
Then they reached both hands to the white starting line, cupping their
fingers so they could balance their bodies securely. "Set," the starter
intoned, drawing the word out. Each runner raised up his body, holding himself suspended with only his feet in the blocks and his fingers
holding him in place.

And then the starter gun went off, and all eight runners blasted from their blocks while the crowd erupted in an explosive roar of encouragement. United States sprinter Tommie Smith was the race favorite, but few knew he was nursing an injured hamstring muscle. His friend and teammate, John Carlos, was considered Smith's chief rival, though many also had their eyes on an Australian runner named Peter Norman, who had set a world record in one of his heats.

Carlos took off flying, establishing a lead that everyone could see. Smith was slower off the blocks, and when the herd of runners began to round the turn and headed into the final stretch, legs churning, arms pumping, it was hard to see anything very clearly. Except that Carlos had two or three steps on everyone.

This was when Smith's body found another, higher gear, where his afterburners seemed to kick in and he speeded up. He passed Carlos easily and accelerated even more. Norman also dug in and moved up onto Carlos's shoulder. When they came to the finish line, Norman lunged forward.

Tommie Smith had won easily, but everyone waited to see who had come in second. Then the scoreboard flashed the results and times and the crowd became even louder: Tommie Smith had established a new world record, becoming the first person to run 200 meters in under twenty seconds (19.83). Peter Norman had edged Carlos for second, setting an Australian national record (20.06), a mark that still stands to this day. John Carlos had taken third.

Tommie Smith, Peter Norman, and John Carlos had run themselves into the Olympic record books, but their day was far from over. Several hours later, the medal ceremony was to be held, and Smith and Carlos were ready for it.

All three men were part of the group of athletes who had recommended canceling or postponing the Games. Smith's and Carlos's views had been so strong and widely known that the U.S. Olympic Committee sent four-time 1936 Olympic gold medalist Jesse Owens to talk to them, hoping he could persuade them not to do anything rash. But both Smith and Carlos knew the medal ceremony would give them their only chance to have their voices heard around the world.

When the three runners emerged from the tunnel for the ceremony, they were given a loud and sustained greeting as heroic sports figures. Then those in the stands closest to the men noticed something unusual.

Avery Brundage's IOC had very strict, some would say iron-fisted, rules about how Olympic athletes had to represent themselves and their countries. One was that each team's uniforms — sweat suits, socks, shoes — must be worn complete and without any form of political statement attached.

Smith and Carlos appeared shoeless, and instead of white socks, they wore black socks to represent black poverty. Smith wore a black scarf around his neck as a symbol of black pride, while Carlos's track-suit was unzipped in solidarity with all blue-collar workers, black and white, in the United States; he also wore a necklace of black beads, "for," as he said later, "those individuals that were lynched, or killed and that no one said a prayer for."

Out of respect for Norman, they had told him what they planned to do before the ceremony. When they asked him what he thought, Norman said simply, "I'll stand with you," explaining that he supported their protest because he objected to his own country's strict segregationist laws that discriminated against people of color. "I thought I would see fear in his eyes," Carlos recalled. "Instead I saw love."

When Norman learned that Carlos had forgotten to bring his black team gloves, he suggested that Carlos wear one of Smith's. In addition, Smith, Carlos, and Norman all wore the badges of the Olympic Project for Human Rights (OPHR), another clear violation of IOC rules.

After the men stepped up on the podium and received their medals, the national anthem of the United States began to play. All three turned to face the area where the flags would be raised. And then, in what is probably the most famous Olympic gesture ever, Smith and Carlos bowed their heads and held high their gloved hands. Norman stood erect, staring straight ahead.

When the music stopped, the stunned crowd was almost completely silent. No one had ever seen such an overt political statement made at the Olympic Games. "You could have heard a frog piss on cotton," Carlos remembered. "There's something awful about hearing [eighty thousand] people go silent, like being in the eye of a hurricane."

The crowd came vocally alive as the three athletes left the field. It started with a drone of boos, followed by objects being hurled at them as well as racial epithets and chants such as "Go back to Africa!" The next day, the *Los Angeles Times* suggested their raised fists were a "Nazi-like salute."

Avery Brundage agreed with the *Times,* somehow forgetting that he had accepted the actual Nazi salute back in 1936. But Brundage wasn't done. He ordered the U.S. Olympic Committee to suspend Smith and Carlos from the team and have them thrown out of the Olympic Village. Brundage explained that these U.S. athletes had violated "the basic principles of the Olympic games," meaning his rules. He couldn't help adding a personal insult: Smith and Carlos had "warped mentalities and cracked personalities." No one messed with Brundage's Games, he wanted everyone, especially the athletes, to know.

Back home most blacks and many whites supported the three athletes' stance. But there were many people who were outraged by what they considered disrespect for the United States and its flag. And while most of the black Olympic athletes supported the protest, not all did. Jim Hines thought the protest hurt his and other black medal winners' ability to earn advertising and endorsement money. "They didn't think it out," he said later. "The demonstration is the most remembered thing of '68. I hate it."

In the United States, both Smith and Carlos found themselves shunned by athletic associations, sponsors, and potential employers. Both received death threats and had to take any job they could get in order to provide for their families. During one winter, Carlos had to chop up his furniture to heat his home. Smith and Carlos continued to run and managed to set records, but they never made it back to the Olympics.

Norman faced even more hostility back in Australia, where conservative media criticized his participation in the protest. Even though he had thirteen race times that should have qualified him for the 1972 Olympics, he was left off the team. Carlos felt deeply sorry for his friend, saying, "Peter was facing an entire country and suffering alone."

Over the years, feelings toward the three began to soften. Avery Brundage retired from running the IOC after the 1972 Olympics, and somewhat more compassionate and open-minded leadership followed. John Carlos was hired to promote the 1984 Los Angeles Olympic Games, while Smith was asked to help coach the U.S. team at the World Indoor Championships.

Norman died suddenly of a heart attack in 2006, all but forgotten by the athletic world. In 2012, Australia formally apologized to Norman's family, with one member of Parliament saying that Norman's gesture "was a moment of heroism and humility that advanced international awareness for racial inequality."

Smith, Carlos, and Norman all paid a price for their political gesture, socially, athletically, and financially. But they did command the attention of hundreds of millions of people around the world and inspired numerous athletes to use their popularity to advance social issues for discussion. Recently, National Football League quarterback Colin Kaepernick knelt on one knee instead of standing while the national anthem played before a game. He did it to protest the racial discrimination of African Americans and other people of color in this

This statue, housed in the National Museum of African American History and Culture, celebrates the three brave protesting medal winners in Mexico City in 1968. Protests by athletes who have the nation's attention have renewed importance a half century after this event.

country. He was roundly criticized for this action, but within weeks fellow teammates joined him in "taking a knee," as did many other NFL players. The practice has since spread, with Olympic gold medalist and now professional soccer player Megan Rapinoe using the gesture to protest discrimination, especially against gay and transgender individuals.

Asked in a 2012 interview if he ever regretted his action, Carlos replied without hesitation. "I had a moral obligation to step up. Morality was a far greater force than the rules and regulations [Brundage and the IOC] had."

Carlos paused a moment, then added, "I had no idea the moment on the medal stand would be frozen for all time." His words now seem more like a prediction than a proud memory. Today in the sports section of the National Museum of African American History and Culture, there is a life-size bronze statue that shows three men in a quiet, thoughtful moment of protest, two with heads bowed and arms raised. Tommie Smith, John Carlos, and Peter Norman not only sprinted into Olympic history; they also brought world attention to the issues of racial inequality and poverty through a simple but brave gesture that made all three forever a part of international history.

THE CODE WARS

LOREE GRIFFIN BURNS

On the afternoon of December 10, 1968, the Stockholm Concert Hall glowed with pomp and royalty. Flowers and soft light cascaded from all four walls of the main hall, perfuming eight hundred gowned and tuxedoed guests and setting the jewels on Queen Louise's tiara ablaze. When trumpeters let loose from the back of the stage, the Swedish royal family rose with the rest of the audience to welcome, by standing ovation, the world's newest Nobel Prize winners. Among the six men ushered to the front of the stage was forty-one-year-old Marshall Nirenberg. He was an American, the youngest of the night's laureates, and he was being honored, along with his colleagues Robert W. Holley and Har Gobind Khorana, for uncovering one of the most well-guarded secrets of living cells: how information hidden in DNA directs the construction of proteins.

Proteins do all the things that living cells need to do. Cells need a rigid skeleton to give them shape, and the protein actin provides it. Cells need to communicate with one another, and do so by pumping proteins, like insulin, into their environment. Cells sometimes need to respond to those environmental messages, and proteins like the insulin receptor help with that. Your fingernails are made of the protein called keratin, and skin color derives in part from the presence of the protein melanin. There are thousands and thousands of proteins in your body, and each one has its own unique and important function. All of these proteins — actin, insulin, insulin receptor, keratin, melanin, and so many others — are made from a simple set of twenty building blocks: the amino acids. To build a protein, amino acids are joined together in a precise order, one at a time and end to end, into long strings. Based on the properties of the individual amino acids, the string will fold in on itself and form a unique three-dimensional structure that allows the final protein to do the things it does. Here's the surprising part: the instructions describing the exact order of amino acids that should go into each protein strand is stored inside a cell's DNA. And Nirenberg had figured out how to read those instructions.

In a humble acceptance speech later on the night of the Nobel celebration, Nirenberg said, "I know that I stand here as a representative of a community of investigators. That it has fallen to me, for a brief moment, to represent us, I am deeply grateful." What few in the swanky banquet hall realized was how cunning the community of investigators he spoke of had been, or how close they'd come to scooping up Nirenberg's prize for themselves. The years leading up to this night had been an all-out race to crack DNA's instructional code. And even Nirenberg knew that the least likely winner had won.

For example, no one would have been surprised if Nirenberg's prize had gone to James Watson and Francis Crick. The cocky young American and his talkative-to-a-fault British colleague had already won a Nobel for their discovery of the structure of DNA. Their double helix was famous the moment it was announced, and it suggested, in Crick's words, "that the sequence of bases in the DNA coded for the sequence of amino acids in the corresponding protein."

What he meant by this was that the four molecules at the heart of a strand of DNA — adenine (A), cytosine (C), guanine (G), and thymine (T) — are joined in an order that has meaning for the cell. Just as proteins are long strings of amino acids joined end to end, DNA is a long string of bases joined end to end. In Crick's view, the bases are simply a coded list of amino acids, a recipe for building proteins. A cell needs only to read the code, add each listed amino acid one by one and voilà!—it has assembled a new protein. Since Crick and Watson knew more about DNA than just about anyone else in the world, many expected they'd be the ones to decipher this code in its bases.

The other person who could have snagged Nirenberg's Nobel was Severo Ochoa. Like Watson and Crick, Ochoa already had a Nobel of his own, which he earned by studying RNA. Like DNA, RNA contains four bases: A, C, G, and, in place of the T, one called uracil (U). Leading a well-staffed laboratory, Ochoa had shown that RNA was involved in making proteins, too. His team was working furiously to figure out the details.

If there was a code hidden in the bases of DNA, was there also a code hidden in the bases of RNA?

Were these codes related?

How did they work?

No one knew for sure yet. But in 1960, Marshall Nirenberg, proud owner of a new job title (independent investigator) and his first laboratory (a single small room at the National Institutes of Health in Maryland), wanted desperately to find out. He'd spent his career studying the transportation of sugar molecules in cells, but now that he was on his own, he was free to study any problem that caught his eye. He'd decided to focus on what he felt was the essential question of the day: how a cell's DNA and RNA dictated the production of its proteins.

Nirenberg believed that "as an independent investigator you are supposed to hit the deck running." He felt he could do that, even as a young researcher working alone in an entirely new field.

"It is suicidal," a colleague warned him.

But Nirenberg didn't listen. His passion to understand how the sequence of bases in DNA could be translated into a protein was much stronger than any fear of failure. He set about learning all he could, dreaming up experiments and tweaking them day and night until they worked.

During his first summer as head of his own research lab, Nirenberg applied to attend a conference on DNA and proteins at the prestigious Cold Spring Harbor Laboratory. Watson and Crick would be there, and probably Ochoa, too. But since none of the people running the conference had ever heard of Marshall Nirenberg, and since he didn't yet have interesting results to share, his application to attend was denied.

Meanwhile, physicists, mathematicians, astronomers, and researchers of all kinds had been writing to Watson and Crick to offer their thoughts on how a genetic code might work. There were so many enthusiastic theories, in fact, that Watson had formed a club. He invited the best of these would-be code crackers to help him and Crick hammer out theories about the code. He called his select group the RNA Tie Club and limited membership to twenty men: one for each amino acid. (Perhaps if there had been more amino acids, a female scientist might have been added to the club?) Members were assigned amino acid code names; Watson became known as "Proline" and Crick as "Tyrosine." Someone designed a ceremonial tie and hired a haberdasher in Los Angeles to make twenty of them. Each RNA Tie Club member would eventually receive a golden tie tack emblazoned with the three-letter abbreviation for his amino acid, too. Watson got a golden PRO and Crick a golden TYR.

Secret status and cliquey shenanigans aside, the RNA Tie Club members did inspire one another. They communicated mostly by handwritten letters, and they came up with insightful new theories about the code and how it might work. Eventually, based heavily on RNA Tie

Club discussions, Crick proposed what he thought might be the most central idea in all of biology. He wrote his idea this way:

$$DNA \rightarrow RNA \rightarrow Protein$$

by which he meant that the information encoded in the bases of DNA could be transferred directly into the bases of RNA. Since DNA is a huge molecule stuck inside a cell's nucleus, and since proteins are built in a cell's cytoplasm, the liquid surrounding the nucleus, this theory was attractive. The DNA code could be copied into RNA in the nucleus, and then the smaller, more nimble RNA molecule could move out of the nucleus and into the cytoplasm, where proteins are made.

While Crick was drawing out his formula and Watson was hip deep in ties and tacks, Nirenberg was doing actual experiments. He had recruited another researcher, Heinrich Matthaei, to his lab, and he focused their combined energies on making cell-free extracts.

A cell-free extract is basically a test tube of cytoplasm. It had been known for some time that one could break open a bunch of cells, collect the liquid inside them, then use this cell-free extract to study the building of proteins. Whatever process produced proteins in intact cells would now produce proteins in the test tube, with the added benefit that scientists could easily add or subtract ingredients from the test tube and so learn how those ingredients impacted the process. For example, one could isolate RNA molecules from cells and add them to a cell-free extract to stimulate the production of proteins. One could also add RNAse, an enzyme that cuts RNA molecules to shreds, to the same extract at the same time . . . and destroy its ability to produce proteins. The resulting theory? RNA was, indeed, a critical part of protein production.

Nirenberg and Matthaei's early work with cell-free extracts was not new or surprising. Like so many scientists before them, they purified RNA from cells, added it to cell-free extracts, and watched the extracts produce proteins. But by 1961, Nirenberg had a whopper of a code-cracking idea. Instead of purifying RNA from cells and adding it to his extracts, Nirenberg decided to make his own RNA. The advantage to using synthetic RNA, of course, was that he would have complete control over the order of the As, Cs, Gs, and Us. He hoped this might help him understand which bases in RNA coded for which amino acids in a protein.

The synthetic RNA Nirenberg chose was simple. It was a long RNA strand made only of the base uracil; because *poly* means many, he called it poly-U. When Nirenberg added poly-U to his cell-free extracts, the extracts produced protein, just as he expected. The result that made Nirenberg's heart race was this: the protein the extracts built contained only a single amino acid, the one called phenylalanine.

Nirenberg suddenly had two things going for him: the first clue to how the genetic code worked, and, because he'd recently been accepted to speak at the Fifth International Congress of Biochemistry in Moscow, a huge stage on which to tell the world about it.

Nirenberg had applied for the conference long before he'd done the poly-U experiment, so his presentation had a ho-hum title that contained no hint of his bombshell discovery. As a result, only thirty-five of the more than five thousand scientists at the conference were in the room when he dropped that bombshell. In a small, windowless classroom, a space crowded with desks and equipped with a projection machine the size of a man, Nirenberg explained his poly-U experiment. When he was finished speaking, thirty-four scientists sat in stunned silence. But one, a Harvard professor named Matthew Meselson, understood exactly what had just happened: some unknown kid was on the way to solving the biggest mystery in science. Meselson rushed to the front of the room and hugged Marshall Nirenberg. (This is not something one sees often at a scientific conference.) Then he ran to find Francis Crick.

. . .

Until Matt Meselson found Francis Crick somewhere on the campus of the Moscow State University on that day and explained what he'd just learned, the RNA Tie Club had never heard of Marshall Nirenberg. Crick realized instantly the importance of Nirenberg's results, though, and went off to speak to the young man himself. After a brief meeting, it was agreed that Nirenberg would share his results again in a hastily arranged second presentation.

This time he spoke in a larger room filled with scientists from all corners of the globe. He repeated the news that an RNA molecule made only of the base uracil prompted a cell-free extract to produce a protein made only of the amino acid phenylalanine. For the second time in a week, Nirenberg's results inspired a grown man to leap from his seat and run from the conference room. This time it was Severo Ochoa.

Ochoa's lab had been trying to understand protein synthesis with cell-free extracts, just like Nirenberg. In fact, one of Ochoa's students had been preparing to use synthetic RNA in the very same way Nirenberg had just described. As soon as he could, Ochoa cabled his team in New York from Moscow. He told them they'd been scooped, that someone had beaten them to the synthetic RNA experiments. He shared all the details he could remember from Nirenberg's talk, and then he told his team to get busy using those details to decipher the rest of the genetic code. Quickly.

A three-way race was now under way. And Nirenberg, undisputed hero of the entire Moscow conference, was not a good bet to win it. The odds were against him and Matthaei beating the RNA Tie Club *and* Ochoa's group, two well-equipped and well-funded teams of researchers. Nirenberg needed to get back to his lab and to his experiments immediately, and he knew it. But he'd been married just days before flying to the Moscow conference!

"I thought that was the worst time in the world to take a vacation," he later said. But take a vacation he did.

Nirenberg's honeymoon lasted two weeks. Luckily the experiments that needed to be done next — making RNA molecules with precise base sequences and feeding them to cell-free extracts to see what amino acids they forced into proteins — were difficult to do. Although scientists knew how to make long strings of RNA containing only a single base, like poly-U, making RNA molecules with specific combinations of all four bases was just not possible yet. All three code-cracking teams — Nirenberg and Matthaei, the dozens of researchers in the Ochoa lab at New York University, and the far-flung members of the RNA Tie Club — struggled to overcome this difficulty. And while Nirenberg didn't have anywhere near the manpower of the other groups, he did have powerful colleagues at his home institution who knew he was on the trail of something important. They were prepared to help him.

His competitors were less helpful. James Watson invited Nirenberg to present his work to an audience at MIT. In a move that he's become infamous for, Watson brought a newspaper along to Nirenberg's presentation and sat in the front row. When he felt Nirenberg was getting boring — or when he wanted Nirenberg to think he was getting boring — Watson snapped open his newspaper and began to read. As if that weren't rude enough, a student from Ochoa's lab showed up at the same talk, and when Nirenberg's presentation ended, the student took the stage and announced his own results! Despite these intimidations, Nirenberg accepted an invitation to visit Ochoa's lab in person. While there, he even offered to collaborate with Ochoa's team, to join forces and resources and work together to crack the remaining words of the genetic code. Ochoa refused.

These experiences were discouraging, but there wasn't much Nirenberg could do. He returned to his lab and dived into his experiments.

"We at NIH were terribly angry with Ochoa and his colleagues for jumping in on Marshall and Heinrich's discovery," wrote NIH researcher Bob Martin. "I tried my best to cheer him up and promised to lend a hand for a few months."

And so an around-the-clock collaboration sprang up at the National Institutes of Health. Nirenberg's progress was slow, but his friends refused to let him despair. When their own work was done for the day, Martin and others helped Nirenberg synthesize RNA and other materials for his experiments. They would hand these supplies off to Matthaei, who used them in experiments he conducted during the night shift. By the time Nirenberg arrived at the lab in the morning, new experimental results were ready for him to analyze. Matthaei went home to sleep while Nirenberg designed a new set of experiments and began the necessary preparations, and by the end of the work day, the entire cycle was ready to begin again. And as months turned into a year, Nirenberg added a few new scientists to his team.

Meanwhile, a clearer model of how proteins are produced was forming in the minds of scientists. It was clear that DNA in the nucleus was used as a template to build an RNA molecule of a precise base sequence, and that this RNA could leave the nucleus. In the cytoplasm, the RNA would bind to protein production machinery capable of reading its base sequence. The next step seemed to be the binding of the first amino acid coded by the RNA in question.

This got Nirenberg wondering.

How much RNA was needed to trigger this first step? In other words, how many bases were needed in order for a strand of RNA to bind the protein production machinery and recruit that first amino acid? The technical detail holding up the code-cracking experiments at this moment was the making of long synthetic RNA strands. Smaller ones would be much easier to make.

So Nirenberg made a couple. He built an RNA strand of only two bases (UU), and another of only three bases (UUU). Then he plugged them into his experiments.

The results were rather incredible.

The two-base RNA, UU, was unable to recruit any amino acids to the protein production machinery. However, the three-base RNA, UUU, recruited the amino acid phenylalanine. It worked exactly as the longer poly-U did.

What did this mean? Well, it suggested that the genetic code worked in three-letter increments, that a three-base stretch of RNA coded for each amino acid in a protein.

Equally exciting, it meant that Nirenberg had created a way to decipher the entire genetic code. By making small RNA strands with every possible three-letter combination, dropping them one by one into cell-free extracts, and watching which of the twenty amino acids each one recruited to the protein production machinery, Nirenberg could

These models represent the cellular molecules involved in the construction of proteins. Inside a cell, the six-base-pair stretch of DNA shown on the left would be transcribed into the six-base RNA shown in the middle, and that RNA would be translated into the tiny protein—just two amino acids long—on the right. In an actual cell, DNA molecules are much longer, as are RNA molecules and proteins.

decipher the entire genetic code. And over the next few years, that's exactly what he did.

Francis Crick would always insist that the "magic circle" of the RNA Tie Club was critical to cracking the code of life. And they were. But on October 16, 1968, it was Marshall Nirenberg who received a call from the Nobel Committee, who stood under a banner made and hung by his friends at NIH ("UUU Are Great!" it read), who raised a glass beaker of champagne into the air, and who toasted the team who had helped him win the code wars.

DOUGLAS ENGELBART

MARC ARONSON

y 1968 links with many of the stories in this book. I was
living in Manhattan and going to the New Lincoln School,
in Harlem. Founded on the idea that students would learn
by doing — creating art, fighting for civil rights and social change — New
Lincoln was deeply committed to racial integration. One day when I
was in tenth grade, a recent graduate came to speak to the class. He
was now at the University of California at Berkeley, where he had been
part of the Free Speech Movement (see the chapters about Paris and
Prague, where Mario Savio and the FSM are mentioned again). He and
other Berkeley students were opposed to what they saw as the mecha-
nizing and militarizing of education — "Do Not Bend, Spindle, Fold, or
Mutilate" they said, subverting a phrase used by IBM in reference to
the punch cards then being used in early computers. Berkeley's student
protests are often seen as the beginning of the college campus side of
the '60s' drive for change — and with our teacher's approval, we were
being invited to join in.

In 1968, I had my chance. New Lincoln was on 110th Street, so
when students took over Hamilton Hall at Columbia, I was just a bit
more than six blocks away. I strolled up, past the apartment where
my immigrant aunt who would only speak in Yiddish shuffled in her

bathrobe and made blintzes for me, and watched the occupation. I wanted to be part of the exciting moment, the drama, the intensity, but I was scared. I was afraid of defying the police, afraid of the feeling of chaos and menace in the air. I wanted to be part of the big change, but I wanted to find my "good revolution": a transformation that felt right for me.

That summer, my fellow senior Tony and I went to Europe. We got on bikes in Amsterdam and set off to cross Holland and Germany to Kiel, where we would catch a ferry to Copenhagen and meet beautiful Danish girls. But that trip kept taking me into the past.

In northern Holland, we stayed with relatives of my aunt's husband, Paul. He had been a gentile but also a leader of the resistance against the Nazis, and a colleague of his had been tortured into betraying him. Paul was caught, given an actual trial, and executed by the Germans. My aunt had then fled to the farm and school where I now sat eating cheese studded with caraway seeds. As Tony and I left Holland and biked across Germany, I kept feeling more and more alienated. I was scared of and angry at the Germans I saw eating lunch and heading out on vacation. I felt very Jewish, thin, and vulnerable on my bike. And so when we took a wrong turn and missed Kiel, Tony found his way to Denmark, while I got a train ticket, sped back to Amsterdam, and took a flight to visit relatives in Israel.

The previous year, the Israelis had won the Six-Day War and taken the old city of Jerusalem. Was *this* my good revolution, to be part of the new, confident, expanded Israel? On the kibbutz where I went to pick pears, the teenage girls kept telling me I belonged there; I belonged in Israel; I could never be safe in America. That just did not sound right to me, and I soon headed home. I wanted to explore Israel's deep past, to be an archaeologist, not a farmer on a kibbutz.

History wove into my life in other ways, too. My mother had been born in Prague, so when the Prague Spring began, it reminded me of

Czech heroes I had been reading about on my own: the twentieth-century prime minister Jan Masaryk and, much earlier, the fourteenth-century religious reformer Jan Hus. Current Czech leader Alexander Dubček, Jan Masaryk, Jan Hus—these seemed like the ideal men of good revolutions. They sought to bring new ideas, new freedoms, new hope to closed societies. (If you are curious about these men and go on to learn more about them, you'll run into an interesting word: *defenestration*. I leave it to you to find it and learn what it means.) I so admired the Czechs and always hoped I had some affinity with them—until the Soviet tanks ended that golden moment.

Back in New York, I headed down to Eighth Street, St. Marks Place, to be part of what seemed to be another form of revolution. The Fillmore East was just a few blocks away, and I went there to see the Beatles movie *Yellow Submarine*. I wanted to be transported, to be changed, to be part of the Age of Aquarius—whether that was in protests such as up at Columbia, or in music, and gurus, and transcendence as down in the East Village. But I was never sure whether the long hair, the bell-bottoms, the Nehru jackets, the hot record albums were quite right for me.

And looking back, I realize that I—that so many of us—missed it. We thought the revolution was in taking to the streets, or taking to violence, or taking to drugs, or taking to meditation, or taking to concerts that were meant to be a new kind of religious experience. But in this chapter, I am going to argue that another and perhaps the most significant revolution was in fact taking place in the San Francisco Bay Area, in a way that was totally invisible to me at the time.

And only now, writing this piece, do I realize what I was seeking, discovering, finding in those searches: my real passion was not for violent revolution, storming buildings, communes, and concerts; it was for history. Years later, when I went back to graduate school and earned a master's and then a doctorate, I was in heaven. My revolution had to do with linking back to the past, and so seeing the present in new ways. That is one discovery I made in writing this essay. The other one, about the real "good revolution" of 1968? You'll find out in the next few pages, where you will meet Douglas Engelbart.

Where It All Began

This book includes stories of assassinations, revolutions, and political convulsions that shook Europe, Asia, and North and South America in 1968. Yet I am claiming here that the 1968 event with perhaps the most long-lasting effects took place when a man with neatly combed hair, speaking in a very soft, controlled, soothing, almost expression-less voice talked about a shopping list—some chores his wife had asked him to do on his way home.

Really.

The day was December 8, 1968, and perhaps one thousand com-puter programmers and engineers, almost all white and male, sat in an auditorium and saw their future—the future we live in today—fore-told. In fact we so take for granted the world unveiled on that date that I have to explain what life was like before the image of Douglas Engelbart's head appeared on a 22-foot screen.

By 1968, the military, NASA, and key universities all knew that computers were getting ever more powerful and should be capable of great things. Which great things? The path that excited most computer scientists was artificial intelligence. And to this day, there are those in Silicon Valley with precisely the same aim—including those who made IBM's Watson a chess and *Jeopardy!* champion. Indeed, some believe that what is called "the singularity"—when computer brainpower matches and surpasses that of humans—is coming soon. In that vision of the future, we are like parents, or perhaps Dr. Frankenstein, creating a new species of silicon-based children. Or to use a slightly different image, humans are like engineers on old locomotives: we shovel data into the mouths of computing machines like coal into a furnace. Since the goal is to create ever more robust machines, we give computers data and commands through strings of text that they can easily handle.

Douglas Engelbart had a different idea.

For decades Engelbart pursued a vision. He believed that people and computers could evolve together. That is, as people developed and used better and better computers, our own minds — our capacity to think — would be "augmented." Indeed, the very process of improving the machines so that they would help us would, in turn, expand human potential. Rather than computers being infant versions of stand-alone artificial intelligence that might surpass our own, humans and computers working together could lead to a faster, greater, enhanced version of the human mind. This co-evolution would take place both for individuals working with computers and for linked groups of people and machines collaborating. Instead of people pouring data into ever bigger and better machines, machines and humans would achieve their mutual potential together.

These two different ways of looking at computing may sound abstract, but for Engelbart's team, this was the most concrete question: What would allow humans to work so closely with computers that in the very process of doing so, the evolution of human intellect would be sped up? On December 8, 1968, the giant face of Engelbart — looking a bit like how you might picture the Great and Powerful Oz — would show the answers they had found. We use those answers every day.

At first the audience could not see Engelbart input information; instead they heard him click a keypad, and the word *word* appeared on the screen. He showed how he could copy and paste it, make rows and paragraphs that could be numbered and further arranged. Ho-hum, you do that every day, right?

Next came the shopping list: Engelbart began with the jumble of fruits and vegetables his wife wanted him to buy, the shoes needing

repair, the overdue library books to return. In a few strokes, he orga-
nized the terms into groups, gave them names, and linked them to
spots on a very simple map of his route home. Okay, you might say,
GPS plus a list—what's so special about that?

When the giant screen split, the audience saw the list and Engelbart
at work. He had a strange setup: to his left a device that looked like a
thumb piano, with five flat rods that performed actions executed by
function keys on a modern computer; a keyboard in the middle; and
to his right a clunky box with a cord. When he moved that box, which
his team had invented and named "the mouse," they all saw the cursor
move across the screen. This was new to everyone.

Instead of the computer being a large object into which Engelbart
fed numbers, it seemed to respond to him. He was performing like a
musician on a pipe organ, his body and mind linking with the computer to produce words.

Next Engelbart demonstrated that you could click on a term and
link from one file to another—and the whole world of hyperlinking
that we now interact with every day was revealed. The screen split
again, and Jeff, working at another location, appeared. Now the two
men shared a document, and two cursors—they called the flicker-
ing points "bugs"—appeared on the screen: think Google Docs. Here,
so far, in one demonstration we had the mouse, links, shared files,
and the entire principle of using a computer by pointing and clicking
instead of by writing strings of commands.

The files the two men were sharing were the actual programming
code used in their project. Just as the team had promised, the very process of building the tools they needed led to new inventions, new tools.
Engelbart called this "bootstrapping": you pull yourself up, and in the
process create the muscles that allow you to pull higher. Since they
were sharing a file, the two men could leave messages for each other
or for others, or search for messages left for them—a kind of e-mail.

There were seventeen people working on this project. As Engelbart came toward the end of his presentation, he mentioned the next step for them: a government division called ARPA was creating a network of linked computers, some twenty or so. Soon he would be able to give this demonstration live on the East Coast through Arpanet, or what today we call the Internet.

In ninety minutes, Engelbart had shown the mouse, linked files, file sharing, split-screen, messaging, and the Internet. In the use of the cursor to create an action by clicking, there was an early stage of GUI—the graphical user interface with which we click on icons to tell the computer what we want done. Seated in the audience—and indeed working on his team—were the inventors who would soon split off to work for Xerox and create the Alto, the small personal computer whose design was copied first by Apple, then by Microsoft in Windows. It was as if Engelbart had landed a space capsule in the nineteenth century and demonstrated the future. In ninety minutes, we left behind the computer as locomotive and entered the world of icons, clicks, and the Net.

You might think, okay, so he and his team invented some computer enhancements—why is that so special? Every day now, there is a new app, a new device. But Engelbart was not just an inventor slightly ahead of his competition. At the very end of his talk, he showed a tiny bit of emotion, and his voice cracked as he thanked his wife and daughters for putting up with his "monomaniacal" pursuit of his dream. He was not exaggerating; he had been like Ahab in *Moby-Dick*, obsessed with his quest. Douglas Engelbart and his team changed the entire model, the entire image, of how people and computers should interact. The inventions were the expression of his vision.

Engelbart created our world but failed to change his. In a way, the spectacular success of his demonstration began his downfall. As his group began to link to others through Arpanet, his tight lab splintered.

His team was made up of skilled, trained computer experts. Some of them could quickly learn how to manipulate the thumb piano, the keyboard, and the mouse. Others found that dance more challenging — but that didn't bother Engelbart. Indeed, he announced that operators would need to master some fifty thousand different commands to make full use of his system. Since his goal was the advancement of human intelligence, he felt that difficult tasks were to be expected and might even serve as useful challenges — the way athletes push their bodies to exhaustion in training, or hobbyists enjoy tackling ever more difficult sudoku puzzles. The user he had in mind was what he called an "intelligence worker."

But a new generation of creators had a different image of who would use the computer. Some pictured the typical computer operator as "Sally" — a secretary accustomed to her typewriter who would want the familiar QWERTY layout and would not want to have to learn the thumb piano device. Others expanded the image of the ideal operator to, well, everybody. Their goal was to make computers "user-friendly" — no augmentation of any sort required. The very capacities that Engelbart showed computers could offer made designers want to create products that would bring the machines to everyone. Some of Engelbart's best engineers — including Bill English, who had made the whole December 8 demonstration work — defected, leaving his lab and joining the group at Xerox that was developing the Alto as a consumer product.

As his role in mapping the future of computing was threatened, Engelbart looked into stranger and stranger sources for his ultimate augmentation plan. The Bay Area was home to a great many people offering supposed pathways to enlightenment through methods such as taking "mind-expanding" drugs, meditating, exploring past lives, screaming your way back to infancy, floating out of your body, contacting UFOs, practicing yoga, fomenting political revolution, becoming an organic farmer, returning to old religions, founding new religions, or utilizing gadgets to "clear" your mind or infuse you with mysterious energies.

Engelbart read the Communist Chinese leader Chairman Mao's Little Red Book (see Lenore Look's chapter on Mao) for ideas on how to reorganize his lab. Then he—and many of his key staff—fell under the influence of a former used-car salesman turned guru who had taken the name Werner Erhard. Erhard's EST (Erhard Seminars Training) combined "attack psychology," designed to confront people with their failings, with the promise that followers (and only followers) could discover their inner essence in a few hyper-intense sessions. The augmentation side of Engelbart's vision fell prey to a pitchman for a cult. By the time Engelbart and his team parted ways with EST—which was under investigation for fraud—the baton of computer innovation had passed first to Xerox and then to Apple. Engelbart went from visionary pioneer to misguided ancestor.

As I see it, there are two or perhaps three lessons from Engelbart's amazing demonstration. The first is about Engelbart himself. His great achievement, the way he pushed personal computing forward, was a product of both his deep understanding of how computers should work *with* people rather than as mere tools, and his conviction that it was possible to transform the human brain. He was a true visionary—one who was perhaps too entranced by his own implausible dream. Maybe pioneers have to be like that: their trust in their own gut instinct is both what allows them to lead where no one else would go *and* what makes it difficult for them to see when they have gone wrong.

Computers have transformed every aspect of our lives and given us ever-better tools for understanding everything from the weirdness of the quantum world to the limits of the universe. But we, the users, are still human. We make the same kinds of mistakes in how we use computer-aided weapons as we did when we only had clubs and spears.

Connected to the Internet by endless devices, we splinter into niches that affirm and reaffirm bias, prejudice, and division. We are not augmented; we are reiterated—me, me, me, me, us, us, us, us, us—all of the time, in so many ways.

The second conclusion I draw is about the present, the past, and the future. While the thousand or so people at the December 8 demonstration—and maybe another couple of thousand computer enthusiasts—knew this was a turning point in their field, at the time it hardly figured in the key events of the year. Anyone else would have said that the subjects of the other chapters in this book (possibly excluding humor) were certain to do more to shape the future than what Engelbart showed on his screen. But while today we *study* the other events of 1968, we *live* in the digital world he made possible. The crises that mean everything in the present may not be the best predictors of what will come to be most significant in the future.

What, then, may be taking place today that only experts in the know recognize as pivotal? What are we not noticing now that may be the seed of the future the world will experience in 2068? Commercial space flight? The death of coral reefs and the melting of polar ice? Robotics? The engineering of embryos? The growing list of distant (and not so distant) planets that seem capable of supporting life? DNA traces of our complex evolutionary ancestry? Bitcoin blockchains? Drones replacing cars? The roads the Chinese are building in Africa? A song? A fashion? Something else entirely? We may not be augmented, but we will be different—how?

My third conclusion is more of an epilogue. When I mentioned this chapter in a faculty meeting at Rutgers, a senior professor told me that he had actually met Engelbart—late in the '90s, when the pioneer was so dishonored that he couldn't even find a computer division to give him an office. And when I shared my sense that Engelbart's demonstration was one of the most influential events of 1968, he raised an important question: How do you weigh technological progress against social progress? Since 1968, untold billions of dollars have been poured into making faster chips, better displays, more robust computers. We can see the effects of that investment in endless generations of new devices. But the influence of the ideals for which Martin Luther King Jr. and Robert F. Kennedy gave their lives, the impact of the dreams of the protesters in Mexico City, Paris, New York, Chicago, and Prague—these are harder to trace.

Perhaps this just shows how mesmerized we are by technology. What if we had put the same national and international effort as was poured into computers into dealing with our social divisions? What if we all still used clunky mainframe computers—and lived in a more just society? That is a question of priorities that you will have to consider over the next fifty years.

AUTHOR NOTES

Jennifer Anthony—"Gym Crow"

I was a weird little kid.

When I spent time at my friends' houses, I would go along with their requests to play house or tag or other fairly normal kid games.

But when friends came to my house, one of my very favorite things to play was "Orphanage." On those afternoons, my entourage of stuffed animals would be recast as orphans, and my friends and I would assume the roles of the orphanage's caretakers and teachers.

From an early age, I had this drive to step outside my own experience, to try to understand and look out for others—people who might be experiencing pain or discomfort or neglect, and do my best to right as many wrongs as I could. I learned—through play and real life—that this wasn't always easy.

Perhaps this drive is what drew me to learn more about the demonstrations at Columbia University in the spring of 1968, when students and community members alike rose up and fought for what they believed in.

I decided to write the piece from the perspective of Columbia University student Mark Rudd, who was protesting numerous issues—some of which had a potential immediate impact on him, such as the Vietnam War (if he were drafted), but also others that affected him indirectly, such as racism and prejudice toward black students and community members. I began my research by reading few books about Rudd's upbringing and experiences. He was eager to right society's wrongs.

Yet he was only one person among many protesters that spring.

I knew that I had to incorporate and understand other people's perspectives, too. So I searched for information in the archives of the university's newspaper, the *Columbia Daily Spectator,* which turned out to have numerous articles and pictures about the protests written by fellow university students. I also tracked down pieces on the subject in prominent newspapers, such as the *New York Times.* And because I soon learned that the media had focused far more on the white students' than the black students' roles and experiences in the demonstration, I sought out information in books and newspaper articles that shared black students' experiences, too.

Finally, because this event took place before I was born, I wanted to ground myself in time and place as best I could, to try to experience the world through the students' and community members' eyes. I studied the photographs in books and newspaper articles to see how students dressed — and looked up the weather that spring to determine how comfortable (or uncomfortable!) they might have been wearing those clothes. I researched other national and global events to see how these events might have influenced peoples' perspectives and thoughts. And I listened to popular songs and albums from that time period, to imagine how the words and melodies might have helped shape them.

Through this process, I learned that even though these events took place before I was born, these people were really not much different from me. They, too, wanted to make the world a better place.

This piece is dedicated to my mom, my first teacher in empathy, compassion, and standing up for myself and others.

Marc Aronson—"Douglas Engelbart"

When I came to what was then Harper & Row in 1987, I made it a condition of my employment that I have a personal computer. That made me the first person in the children's book department to have one. Until that point, editors communicated with authors and agents in letters written on typewriters. Each letter was "backed up" by a carbon copy. The copies were gathered in "circ" (circulation) files and shared around the office. A young assistant editor would wade through these ghostly pages — seeing a great number of minor notes and, occasionally, the kind of master class in editorial communication that Leonard Marcus gathered in *Dear Genius,* the editorial correspondence of Ursula Nordstrom with artists such as Maurice Sendak and Shel Silverstein. While she was no longer at Harper, her stamp could still be felt in some of the letters we read.

I mention this to show that I experienced the personal computer revolution first as a user. Only later, when I wrote a biography of Bill Gates, did I start to study it as a research topic. I came to write about Gates as I was also writing about other larger-than-life figures — often complex people who were both great and deeply flawed: heroes and antiheroes at the same time. Those books included *Sir Walter Ralegh and the Quest for El Dorado; Robert F. Kennedy;* and *Master of Deceit: J. Edgar Hoover and America in the Age of*

Lies. Another thread in my books has been the idea of revolution in various fields — art: *Art Attack: A Short Cultural History of the Avant-Garde;* world history: *The Real Revolution: The Global Story of American Independence;* and in two books cowritten with my wife, Marina Budhos — agriculture: *Sugar Changed the World: A Story of Magic, Spice, Slavery, Freedom, and Science;* and photojournalism: *Eyes of the World: Robert Capa, Gerda Taro, and the Invention of Modern Photojournalism.* I enjoy exploring passionate personalities, pioneers, and moments of change — which leads to this book.

While researching my Gates book, I read John Markoff's *What the Dormouse Said: How the Sixties Counterculture Shaped the Personal Computer Industry* (New York: Viking, 2005), which explores the unexpected overlap between the New Age/hippie experiments of the '60s Bay Area and the computer science breakthroughs taking place in the same region, often involving the same people. His book introduced me to Engelbart and his famous demonstration. Markoff is a lively, clear writer who recounts many entertaining and informative stories. The book is worth dipping into to get a flavor of the time and place. I reread Markoff for this book, but then dived far more deeply into the Engelbart story through Thierry Bardin's *Bootstrapping: Douglas Engelbart, Coevolution, and the Origins of Personal Computing* (Stanford: Stanford University Press, 2000). The book is quite academic and can be slow going. But it includes a rich selection of interviews, including some with Engelbart and personal accounts from those who worked with him. Bardin knows his subject extremely well, so this is an ideal resource for the dedicated reader who wants to explore Engelbart and this early phase of personal computer history more fully.

Once I understood the context of the December 8 event, I went to Stanford University's MouseSite Digital Archive and watched the actual demonstration (http://web.stanford.edu/dept/SUL/library/extra4/sloan/mousesite/1968 Demo.html). I found it more useful to see the whole event, stopping periodically to read in Bardin to make sure I understood what I was seeing, than to take the option of viewing discrete five-minute segments. The rest of the site also contains useful links and contextual information.

Susan Campbell Bartoletti—"People, Get Ready"

I turned ten in November 1968. Still, all these years later, I can remember the awe I felt at my friends' older brothers and sisters who wore long hair and flower-power clothing and strung beads from the doorway of their dark, incensed-infused bedrooms.

I remember hearing older kids talk about the "true meaning" of "Puff the Magic Dragon." Today, I can't listen to Bob Dylan's "Blowin' in the Wind" and Pete Seeger's "If I Had a Hammer" without recalling how we sang them at church camp.

I remember watching on television the news about the murders of MLK and RFK, the riots, and the Chicago convention, the nightly Vietnam War body count, the antiwar protests and student demonstrations. I remember reading about these things in the daily newspaper.

One night at the dinner table, I said to my mother, "I don't know if I want to go to college to learn or to demonstrate."

No doubt about it: the '60s informed me and helped to shape me into the writer I am today. I've written about child labor (*Growing Up in Coal Country* and *Kids on Strike!*), famine (*Black Potatoes: The Story of the Great Irish Famine, 1845–1850*), the nearly nine million children and teenagers who followed Adolf Hitler (*Hitler Youth: Growing Up in Hitler's Shadow*), the men who joined a secret terrorist group that took root in America's democracy (*They Called Themselves the K.K.K.: The Birth of an American Terrorist Group*), an early-twentieth-century domestic cook named Mary Mallon who suffered human and civil rights violations (*Terrible Typhoid Mary: A True Story of the Deadliest Cook in America*), and now, Abbie Hoffman and the Yippie movement.

Ah, Abbie. I didn't intend to write about Abbie. But the more I read about him and the way he toyed with the media, the public, politicians, and the law, the more parallels I saw to today's current political climate, with its twenty-four-hour news cycles, fake news, alternative facts, clickbait headlines, social media, and conspiracy theories.

What writer, what student of history, can resist exploring such parallels? Aren't we always asking how the past reaches into the present? If the past is ever truly past? If history repeats itself? If we're doomed to repeat the lessons we haven't mastered from the past? Or if the present affects the way we remember the past?

What did your grandparents and great-grandparents wear in their hair during the summer of 1968? You might want to ask.

Loree Griffin Burns—"The Code Wars"

I spent my twenties in a research lab trying to understand how animal cells regulate the expression of the genes in their DNA. After six years of experiments, I'd earned a doctoral degree and developed what felt like an intimate relationship with DNA. I'd learned to collect it from living cells (in my case, yeast cells), study it with sophisticated biological tools, and manipulate it in astonishing ways. I could cut a DNA strand, glue it to a DNA fragment of my own choosing, return the final product to the inside of living cells, and in so doing, change the way those cells functioned. I did this sort of thing daily and, honestly, without too much effort. Modern-day molecular biology of this kind is routine, if incredible, and allows scientists to ask and answer questions about how specific DNA sequences work, how broken ones don't work, and even how to fix them. I was so busy using DNA, though, that there wasn't much time to appreciate the molecule itself, or the long line of scientists who'd figured out how it worked.

When I left bench work to make my way as a writer, I finally turned to this history. Partly because I was curious, and partly because of a meeting I'd had just before leaving the research field. It happened during a three-week residency at the prestigious Cold Spring Harbor Laboratory in New York—where Marshall Nirenberg had learned bacterial genetics and where he was later denied an opportunity to share his early code work. One night, after finishing up in the lab, I took a walk around campus. I turned onto a shrubby footpath toward the ocean, and at its end I came upon an older guy, standing alone and looking out over the water. He was in shorts and tennis shoes, and his mop of gray hair gave him away before he even turned around. It was James Watson. I have impressions of what happened next, remembered feelings (paramount of these was nervousness), but no memory of our actual conversation. I know for sure it was short. Awkward. Over before it began, really. I believe it was the moment I started thinking about this story.

Omar Figueras—"Student Sacrifices"

When initially thinking about the events in Mexico City in 1968, I remembered Tommie Smith's and John Carlos's famous Black Power salutes at the Olympics. I wanted to focus, however, on the Mexicans. What was their attitude toward the games, and toward their government's unwillingness to listen to its people?

Much like an archaeological excavation, the more I dug into this soil, the more valuable was the information I found. The story of Mexican citizens at this time was a story that needed retelling and should never be forgotten. It was the past speaking into the present, and a foreboding echoing of what atrocities a government is capable of committing against its young people. It was Mexico's Kent State, its Tiananmen Square.

Despite the news reports, books, archival footage, and film that emerged in the years that followed, I couldn't conceive of how almost half a century later, this tragedy has been seemingly swept under the rug. Although it's commemorated in Mexico, few people outside the country know of this horrible event. Encountering Elena Poniatowska's seminal text, *Massacre in Mexico*, I found myself haunted by the stories within it. I can still hear these voices, crying, calling out to me. I can only hope that I have done them justice in retelling their tale and that others will listen.

When I'm not writing fiction and nonfiction, I'm teaching English composition, literature, and creative writing at Miami Dade College, in Florida. I hold an MFA in writing from Spalding University, in Louisville, Kentucky.

Paul Fleischman—"Biker's Ed"

Assassinations, elections, riots, shocking news from the war in Vietnam. Nineteen sixty-eight was written in big-font headlines. But some events unfurl too slowly to appear as headlines, or to make it into newspapers at all. I chose one of those, a change in the *zeitgeist*—a German term for the spirit of an era. Instead of bullets, there were books, song lyrics, and movies gradually turning the culture toward the idea that money might not be the greatest good, that life was meant to be a quest, not an endlessly repeated commute.

I had no idea at the time that my two-wheeled quest was preparing me for a lifetime as a writer, but it was. With tent, sleeping bag, and food, bikers are self-contained and independent. They choose and change their routes. They're mobile, seeing something new every day. I lead a similar life as a freelance writer. I'm no one's employee and am free to follow my interests wherever they lead. I love writing's variety and have worked in many genres. I thrive on chance and serendipity, just as travelers do. I never know what's around the next bend.

Biking not only showed me how to lead the writing life, but it also gave me some of my material. From *The Birthday Tree*—my first book—to *Whirligig,*

Breakout, and *The Matchbox Diary,* many of my works are built around journeys. The ever-present past around me in New England kindled not only historical fiction like *Bull Run* but also *Dateline: Troy* and *Eyes Wide Open,* books that cast a historical eye on the present. My collections of two-voiced poems about birds and insects grew out of my years in the New Hampshire woods.

Quests aren't pleasant vacations. Between books, I'm often lost, unsure which way to head next. There's no map to show me the way. I've followed plenty of roads that turned out to be dead ends. You can get similarly lost in a particular book. Dense fog, flat tires, and washed-out bridges are common. Writing isn't a job for anyone who craves certainty or arriving on time.

But if you begin meeting those obstacles at a young age—say, sixteen—and continue gaining experience getting past them—say, by riding a thousand miles or so—you might do just fine.

Laban Carrick Hill—"The Wrong Side of History"

This is the first time I've written about growing up in the South during the civil rights movement. My family began on the wrong side of history, but my immediate family—my mother, my sister, and myself—eventually took up the civil rights standard and have become dedicated to rights for all. My mother was treasurer on the original board of the National Civil Rights Museum at the Lorraine Motel in Memphis, and, as a banker, she secured the initial loans to build the museum. I have spent most of my life coming to terms with race in America.

Over the years, I have published more than forty books, including the National Book Award Finalist *Harlem Stomp! A Cultural History of the Harlem Renaissance* and the Caldecott Honor and Coretta Scott King Illustrator Award winner *Dave the Potter: Artist, Poet, Slave.*

Mark Kurlansky—"Robert F. Kennedy" and "Prague Spring"

I was born in Hartford, Connecticut. I started pursuing both theater and journalism in high school and majored in theater at Butler University's college of performing arts. After college, I had several plays produced in New York and worked many jobs, including commercial fisherman, cook, pastry maker, and paralegal. I then worked for fifteen years as a newspaper correspondent based in Paris and in Mexico City and reporting all over the world.

Since 1992, I have had thirty books published, including three for children and three for young adults. My books for young people have won awards from the American Library Association and National Parenting Publications.

Among my adult books, several have been bestsellers, and I have won diverse awards including the Dayton Literary Peace Prize and the James Beard Award. My books have often drawn on, or woven together, themes from many different parts of the world, as in *Cod: A Biography of the Fish That Changed the World, Salt: A World History, Paper: Paging Through History,* and *International Night: A Father and Daughter Cook Their Way Around the World* (with Talia Kurlansky).

My work has been translated into more than twenty-five languages. I first explored the theme of this book in my own *1968: The Year That Rocked the World.* Tackling the entire year on my own, I explored and wove together stories from Europe, North and South America, and Asia.

I was a college student in 1968, and the year had a huge impact on my life. In writing for this anthology, I called on my own memories of working for Bobby Kennedy as well as the research I did for my adult book.

Lenore Look—"The Red Guard"

The year 1968 was an eventful year in my own life. I had just begun kindergarten in the fall of 1967, and sometime before my youngest brother was born, in January 1969, our family exploded—unannounced, at least to me—when my *pohpoh* and three uncles arrived from Hong Kong and moved into our small, three-bedroom house in Seattle. I was unaware that people were fleeing China in record numbers, but I had some sense from their tense, nightly conversations that pulled at the seams of my dreams until the wee morning hours, that there were things that had been irretrievably lost. For the next several years—exactly how long it lasted, I'm not sure—our lives were swept up in the activities and anxieties of endless job searches and cycles of unemployment for all the newcomers. During this time, one of those uncles sexually molested me, and again, I have no idea of the exact duration, but I was so isolated and terrorized by it that by the time I was in the sixth grade, I wanted to take my own life.

When I was asked to contribute to this volume, I did not see the connection between the abuse I endured and the events in China. The revolution was someone else's history. The suffering happened far away. It was only when I wrote the words "the hard lives of children during the Cultural Revolution" that I realized I was one of them. History is personal. Events far from our homes, and even centuries before our own lifetimes, affect us in profound ways every day. It was only when I allowed myself to write from my inner difficulties, instead of without them, that I found a moment of heightened clarity and mindfulness, and perhaps a deeper gaze into events that touched us all.

I began my research by looking at the period just before Mao Zedong came to power, to help me think about the Cultural Revolution in its historical context. *The Rape of Nanking* by Iris Chang (New York: Basic, 2011) was particularly helpful. I also read online the archived speeches and writings of Mao, and an online translation of his Little Red Book. In China, the '60s was a decade without books, without literature, except for Mao's publications and the criticism posters.

In terms of how to think about China, the revolution, and Chinese sensibilities without the Schadenfreude so often present in western viewpoints, the best book I found was *China in Ten Words* by Yu Hua, translated by Allan H. Barr (New York: Pantheon, 2011). Other helpful books and memoirs I read are listed in the source notes.

Additionally, I read excerpts from Confucius's *Analects,* because the last 2,500 years of Chinese culture is said to be based on Confucian philosophy. I discovered that he taught loyalty to the government first, before loyalty to parents. Ironically, Red Guards desecrated his burial place in Qufu, Shandong Province.

Finally, I read Laozi, who died twenty years before Confucius was born. He founded the philosophy of Daoism, which urges practicing simplicity and following the life force. In verse 58, Laozi offers advice, yet unheeded: When a government rules with a light hand, people are productive. When the government is tyrannical, the people rebel. When the bad fortune of many supports the good fortune of a few, it is injustice.

Who can tolerate the injustice? Without limits, the hypocrisy never ends.

David Lubar—"Running with Sharp Schticks"

Comedy and I go way back. In 1961, when I was seven, I made the thrilling discovery that a person could earn a living writing jokes. My revelation came by way of *The Dick Van Dyke Show,* a TV series about a character named Rob

Petrie, who wrote sketches for a fictional comedy program. By that point in my life, I was constantly making jokes, or at least statements that resembled jokes structurally, though their content often amused only me and frequently puzzled or annoyed whichever adult I happened to interrupt when I blurted out my material. (The interrupted adult was often a teacher, which is why I am amazed that teachers now invite me to speak to their students. This is also why I try not to get annoyed when a student interrupts me with a joke. I just figure it's me coming back to haunt myself.)

All through the 1960s, I devoured comedy shows and worshipped people like Red Skelton, who performed sketches about the quirky characters he'd created, and Jonathan Winters, who could take a piece of wood, a wallet, a cheese grater, or any other common object and instantly improvise hilarious scenes. In my search for humor, I discovered, to my delight and to the dismay of all those within earshot, that the library had joke books. Yes, there were whole books filled with jokes that I could memorize and share with my classmates! I was also a fan of comic strips, cartoons, song parodies, and *Mad* magazine. As I grew older, I focused on stand-up as my comedy of choice.

Despite all this interest, I did not become a comic or a modern-day Rob Petrie. But I am fortunate to have found another way to make people laugh: through my novels and short stories. Given my passion for humor, it's no surprise that when I was asked to write an article about 1968, comedy came to mind and stand-up took center stage. Add in the fact that 2017 (and also 2018) has a good chance of taking a gold or silver medal in the race to become one of the most turbulent years I've experienced, standing side by side with the rock tumbler that was 1968, and the topic of humor as a weapon for social change seemed irresistible.

But there's a big gap between the ease of saying, "Sure, I'll write a piece for the book," and the reality of doing the work. I couldn't just sit down and start writing. Given that I'm not sure what I had for breakfast yesterday, it seemed risky to trust my recollections from half a century ago. So I had the pleasure of doing research. I watched old shows and documentaries, read old newspaper and magazine articles, listened to comedy albums, and sampled biographies. I had already read George Carlin's bio and many books about comedy writers, but while wandering the library in search of inspiration, I was delighted to discover Gerald Nachman's *Seriously Funny: The Rebel Comedians of the 1950s and 1960s* (New York: Pantheon, 2003). In addition to that book and the sources listed in the notes, I also devoured David

Bianculli's *Dangerously Funny: The Uncensored Story of The Smothers Brothers Comedy Hour* (New York: Simon & Schuster, 2009).

So I had a topic and a ton of material. Fortunately, I also had two experienced nonfiction writers as editors who helped me shape my somewhat unfocused first draft into the tightly crafted essay included in this book. And, best of all, I had a lot of fun revisiting the transformational comedy of my youth and finding the right words to share that experience with you. Peace, my friends.

Wait. There's one more thing I need to tell you, because I'm still that seven-year-old kid who desperately wants to share my jokes with the world and earn your approval. Several years ago, I had the chance to take a class in stand-up comedy. It was a wonderful experience, and I learned a lot. We had to give a graduation performance. To see how that turned out, search for "David Lubar stand-up" on YouTube.

Okay. Now I'm finished. Carry on.

Kate MacMillan—"The Student View from Paris"

I am currently a school district librarian in northern California with six grandchildren. When I was approached to write the student view, I hesitated because it was so long ago. It took me a few months of talking to very old friends and reading old and often inaccurate newspaper articles online to jog my memory back fifty years. After all, we knew then that we could not really trust anyone over the age of thirty . . . and most reporters were older than that.

I was a radicalized sorority girl from an upper-middle-class California family. From being part of the surfing world to being a young artist to joining Students for a Democratic Society, I was on the fringe. But I can't write just about myself, because we were a group and in our memories, we are forever intertwined.

What was it about that year? We had lived through the famous Summer of Love, and we all fell in love with our music and the person of the moment. But 1968 was unique. There was something in the air that was edgy and different. When Paris beckoned, we went without a thought. Was it fun? In the beginning, it was exciting, but then it became uncomfortable, dirty, and mean. By the end of May, there was still passion and belief, but most of us were out of money and out of our depth. The party was over.

Some of us continued to demonstrate against Vietnam; some were consumed by the draft lottery; some became even more radicalized. But like most, I finished college and got married, had children and lived a quiet life. But I still held onto my liberal beliefs.

Even after all this time, I will always remember 1968 as the year that touched every one of us in different ways. Some lived to regret their part in it, while some still believe that they made an important impact. I believe that it changed my life and gave me the courage of my convictions to speak against injustice, racism, and intolerance. As one of the *soixante-huitards,* I have been forever touched for the better by these experiences.

Kekla Magoon—"The Death of the Dream"

Even before writing this essay, I'd spent a great deal of creative energy contemplating the year 1968. I've written two novels—*The Rock and the River* and *Fire in the Streets*—featuring young teens joining the Black Panther Party in 1968 Chicago. I'm teased by the historical question of what it might have been like to live in this place and time, and who I might have become—a civil rights organizer? A Black Panther? A bystander too terrified to act? These two novels explore a critical moment in American history, the same moment I've addressed in this essay. The assassination of the Reverend Dr. King marked a shift in the civil rights movement, as young people lost patience with and faith in passive resistance as an organizing strategy, and looked for new avenues to channel their rage, frustration, and desire to create change. Too often we speak about the civil rights movement in simplistic terms, and through my historical writing I strive to draw out the deep complexities of the past, and inspire readers to feel the emotional weight of those struggles.

The struggle continues, of course, beyond this particular moment in history. There is always a way to look deeper, and I write hoping to inspire my readers to become more engaged in creating social change in their own communities. *X: A Novel* (written with Ilyasah Shabazz) tells the story of teenage Malcolm X. Before he became the man we remember and celebrate, he was a lost, confused boy who had no idea that he had the potential to become a leader of millions. His story shows the importance of taking small steps to make change, even when you feel like you can't make a difference—because what if you can? *How It Went Down* explores the controversial shooting of a black teen by a white man through multiple viewpoints, challenging the reader to engage with what is uncertain and form a viewpoint of their own. I reach for untold stories and new perspectives as much as possible. I've written several contemporary novels featuring biracial girls: *Camo Girl, 37 Things I Love,* and the Robyn Hoodlum Adventures series, which reimagines the classic character of Robin Hood as a biracial teenage girl in an urban setting.

My work has been well received, garnering an NAACP Image Award, two Coretta Scott King Honors, a Walter Dean Myers Honor, and a National Book Award Long List inclusion. I'm pleased by these recognitions in part because they indicate that at least one corner of society is ready to engage in difficult conversations and reflections on who we are, who we have been, and who we might become, not just as individuals but as a community.

I graduated from Northwestern University with a BA in history, then Vermont College of Fine Arts with an MFA in writing. I now teach in the low-residency MFA in Writing for Children and Young Adults program at Vermont College of Fine Arts.

Jim Murphy—"Running into History"

In 1968, I was a student at Rutgers University, in New Jersey. I read a great deal—newspapers, magazines, and books—plus I absorbed television and radio news broadcasts. I was surrounded by and immersed in the events taking place in the United States and in the world beyond our borders.

I felt it was a time of anger and hope, of protest and counterprotest, when individuals and groups with little or no power raised their voices to demand their rights, and where many who actually held power did everything they could to stifle these cries for justice and maintain their established positions. The country and the world seemed on the verge of chaos, revolution, and collapse or, possibly, on the threshold of a new and better era.

But why did I ask to write about the Black Power salute given at the Olympic medal ceremony for the 200-meter race? Well, to begin with, I was a sprinter in high school and at Rutgers, and I was pretty good at it, being part of two national championship relay teams, making the finals and medaling in the national 60-yard dash, and winning twenty or so state champion medals in both sprints and relays.

I wasn't good enough to make the 1968 Mexico Olympics, but I met and ran with a number of the athletes who did. For instance, that national 60-yard dash was won by Jim Hines (who would go on to set world records and win Olympic gold in 1968); I worked out several times with long jumper Ralph Boston (who won gold in the 1960 Olympics, silver in 1964, and bronze in 1968); and our mile relay team helped pace distance runner Marty Liquori in workouts for several months (at age nineteen in 1968 in Mexico, Liquori was the youngest person to reach the 1,500-meter finals). None of these people remember me, but I recall with a certain amount of pride running with and against them.

The 1968 Mexico Olympics are remembered for many things, but the most controversial moment came when Tommie Smith and John Carlos raised their gloved hands to give the Black Power salute. I knew a good deal about this gesture of defiance and outrage, mainly because I watched it happen on television and followed the resulting controversy that ensued. When I started digging around for more information, I learned details I hadn't been aware of, especially about the steep price both Smith and Carlos paid for years for their belief in human dignity and justice. And then there was that third person on the awards podium, Australian Peter Norman, who went largely unnoticed at first but who helped Smith and Carlos carry out their protest and who suffered as much harsh criticism as his two fellow athletes, all because he believed in the human rights of all people. There are lessons to be learned from this long-ago moment that might come in handy in today's often loud, confusing, and contentious world.

I left the world of serious running long ago, only to wind up in a career that's, no kidding, even more competitive and challenging: writing books for young people.

So far I've managed to write more than forty books, most of them narrative nonfiction dealing with historical topics, that include *The Great Fire, An American Plague,* and *Blizzard!*

You can find several versions of both the 1968 Olympics men's 200-meter final and the awards ceremony for it on YouTube.

Elizabeth Partridge—"Nightly News"

In 1968, my hometown of Berkeley, California, was an exhilarating, frightening epicenter of protest, combustion, and rage. I was in high school, and across the Pacific Ocean to the west lay Vietnam. To the east, on the far side of the United States, stood the White House, where rapid-fire decisions were being made by the president. We rarely talked in eleventh grade about jobs after high school or college campus tours: we were up against the military draft. Every eighteen-year-old male out of high school could be drafted, unless he was deferred. My friends endlessly debated the best ways to avoid the draft.

Berkeley High School was huge. There were more than three thousand students, many with astonishing political savvy, laced with frustration and despair. Being in an urban area, the tensions of society were right there with us in the classrooms and corridors. We routinely poured out of high school and cut classes to march on the streets. We saw no other way to protest: the voting age was twenty-one, which seemed light-years away. In the spring of 1968, people reacted with shock to the deaths of Martin Luther King Jr. and Robert Kennedy. As neighborhoods across the United States went up in smoke, spontaneous interracial brawls broke out on campus.

We had three nightly television news broadcasts: ABC, CBS, and NBC. They kept us current with reports from Vietnam, including daily recitations of American combat deaths, "body counts" of enemy dead, and occasional mention of Vietnamese civilian deaths. These numbers, delivered so dispassionately by the news anchor, horrified me. They came relentlessly, rising and falling with ambushes and battles, downed airplanes and massacres. So much suffering and loss reduced to numbers.

To capture the staccato feeling of the casualty numbers, I included a monthly casualty report in "Nightly News." I relied on the American War Library website, http://www.americanwarlibrary.com/vietnam/vwc24.htm, which cites numbers compiled by the Department of Defense in 1979. Since then, the numbers for Americans have been revised slightly, but I was concerned about the numbers for enemy and civilian dead, which are difficult to account for in any war. In the Vietnam War, some of these assumed enemy dead were without doubt civilians, as enemy body counts were considered evidence that we were winning the war. When I tried to double-check the numbers through the National Archives, the chief of Textual Reference Operations responded that the paper records they had were "extremely voluminous and unprocessed" (personal e-mail, July 27, 2017). Those buried, unprocessed numbers feel symbolic of the many ways we haven't wanted to look back at our part in the Vietnam War.

My high-school years and the nightly news broadcasts profoundly shaped me. For "Nightly News," I needed a writing form that would allow me to pull from deep in my bone marrow rather than standing at a safe distance. I began with a pencil and paper and let memories rise up, capturing their essence and then shaping them into a prose poem.

As it did in "Nightly News," a mix of politics, music, art, protest, and conflict often grabs my attention and makes me want to research and write. My books include *Marching for Freedom: Walk Together, Children, and Don't You Get Weary; Restless Spirit: The Life and Work of Dorothea Lange; Dogtag Summer;* and *This Land Was Made for You and Me: The Life and Songs of Woody Guthrie.* My most recent book is *Boots on the Ground: America's War in Vietnam.*

SOURCE NOTES

pp. 3–5, 30–31, 76–77, 116–119: The statistics given throughout the "Nightly News" pieces are from "Vietnam War Deaths and Casualties by Month," American War Library website, November 27, 2008, http://www.americanwarlibrary.com/vietnam /vwc24.htm. See further discussion in the author's note, pages 177–178.

The Red Guard by Lenore Look

p. 15: "Chairman Mao often says . . . these cultural spheres": "Circular of the Central Committee of the Communist Party of China on the Great Proletarian Cultural Revolution," May 16, 1966, Marxists Internet Archive: Mao Zedong, accessed June 19, 2017, https://www.marxists.org/subject/china/documents/cpc/cc_gpcr.htm.

p. 15: "four olds": The idea of "four olds" came from Mao, but was defined further by his defense minister Comrade Lin Biao as "sweep away all ghosts and monsters in our society . . . break the old ideas, culture, customs and habits of the exploiting classes and foster the new ideas, culture, customs and habits of the proletariat." Comrade Lin Biao's Speech at the Celebration Rally. Lin Biao. Delivered October 1, 1966. https://www .marxists.org/reference/archive/lin-biao/1966/10/01.htm. The official title of the campaign in Chinese characters was "Destroy the Four Olds, Cultivate the Four News." It first appeared in August 1966 and became the definitive slogan of the Cultural Revolution.

p. 16: "The occupied Sorbonne . . . that attracts them": Mavis Gallant, "The Events in May: A Paris Notebook," *New Yorker*, September 14, 1968, 58.

p. 17: "It's a surprise to know . . . stories to you": name withheld, e-mail to the author, November 7, 2016.

p. 17: "You can't use . . . *'hong weibing'* " and "You must say . . . influence on his life": Nancy Kremers, telephone interview by the author, December 5, 2016.

p. 18: "History has shown . . . the whole people": "Resolution on Certain Questions in the History of Our Party Since the Founding of the People's Republic of China," June 27, 1981, Chinese Communism Subject Archives, Marxists Internet Archive, accessed July 26, 2017, https://www.marxists.org/subject/china/documents/cpc /history/01.htm.

p. 18: "cleavage . . . understanding," and "made the authoritative . . . Cultural Revolution": "Society Firmly Rejects Cultural Revolution," *Global Times*, May 17, 2016, https://www.globaltimes.cn/content/9833735.shtml.

p. 18: four memoirs: Nien Cheng, *Life and Death in Shanghai* (New York: Grove, 1986); Ji-li Jiang, *Red Scarf Girl* (Austin: Holt, Rinehart and Winston, 2002); Shen; Rae Yang, *Spider Eaters* (Berkeley: University of California Press, 1997); Fan Shen, Gang of One (Lincoln: University of Nebraska Press, 2004).

p. 19: "Fearless Red Rebels" and "Great Wall Team": Shen, 31, 30.

p. 20: "I was in kindergarten . . . second-floor window" and "It stole my education . . . person today": Fan Chen, interview by the author, Seattle, WA, December 21, 2016.

p. 21 caption: "Every Communist . . . of a gun'": Mao Zedong, *Quotations from Chairman Mao Tsetung*, 2nd ed., Peking: Foreign Languages Press, 1972, 61.

p. 22: "Just ask for anyone . . . as teenagers" and "Don't mention . . . them bring it up": Jeffrey Chen, interview by the author, New York, NY, February 3, 2017.

p. 22: "We were not allowed to attend school": Lisa Szeto, interview by the author, New York, NY, February 10, 2017.

p. 24: "In China education . . . have had no education": Mao Zedong, "Report on an Investigation of the Peasant Movement in Henan," March 1927, Mao Zedong Reference Archive: Selected Works, Marxists Internet Archive, accessed April 7, 2017, https://www.marxists.org/reference/archive/mao/selected-works/volume-1/mswv1_2.htm.

p. 24: "I went from village . . . good for them": Pui Look, telephone interview by the author, January 14, 2017.

p. 25: "They will fight. No discussion": name withheld, interview by the author, Shanghai, China, May 23, 2017.

p. 34: "We will be in Chicago. . . . Do it!": quoted in David Farber, *Chicago '68* (Chicago: University of Chicago Press, 1994), 17.

Nightly News—Spring by Elizabeth Partridge

p. 39: "Is everybody okay?" and "Don't lift me": quoted in Tye, 436.

The Death of the Dream by Kekla Magoon

p. 40: "Do they know about Martin Luther King?" and "I have some very sad . . . Memphis, Tennessee": "Robert F. Kennedy's Martin Luther King Jr. Assassination Speech," YouTube, 0:01 and 0:14, posted November 23, 2010, https://www.youtube.com/watch?v=BCrx_u3825g.

p. 41: "In this difficult day . . . compassion, and love": ibid., 0:50.

p. 43: "Why should they ask . . . simple human rights?": "Read It: Muhammad Ali's Inspirational Statement on Why He Wouldn't Fight in Vietnam," *New York Daily News,* June 4, 2016, http://www.nydailynews.com/sports/more-sports/muhammad -ali-statement-wouldn-fight-vietnam-article-1.2661120.

p. 44: "Land, bread, housing . . . justice and peace": "Black Panther Party Ten-Point Platform and Program, 1966," History Is a Weapon website, accessed July 10, 2017, http://www.historyisaweapon.com/defcon1/bpp.html.

pp. 45–46: "For those of you . . . by a white man": "Robert F. Kennedy's Martin Luther King Jr. Assassination Speech," YouTube, 1:04, posted November 23, 2010, https://www .youtube.com/watch?v=BCrx_u3825g.

p. 46: "We've had difficult times . . . end of disorder": ibid., 3:56.

Gym Crow by Jennifer Anthony

p. 60: the leaflets told . . . : Rudd, 51–52; George C. Keller, "Six Weeks That Shook Morningside," *Columbia College Today,* Spring 1968, 12, http://www.college.columbia .edu/cct_archive/cct_spring_1968.pdf.

p. 61: "fired up with revolutionary fervor": quoted in Kurlansky, 193.

p. 61: Later, he would admit that he was afraid . . . : Rudd, 52.

p. 61: "committed to a policy of racism": quoted in Stern, 1.

p. 61: "committing a moral . . . King's memory": ibid.

p. 61: "steals lands from the people of Harlem": quoted in Kurlansky, 196.

p. 61: "We will therefore protest against this obscenity": quoted in Stern, 1.

p. 61: "Shame" and "This is a church": ibid.

p. 61: "Blasphemy": quoted in Keller, "Six Weeks That Shook Morningside," *Columbia College Today,* Spring 1968, 12, http://www.college.columbia.edu/cct_archive/cct _spring_1968.pdf.

p. 62: "Reply to Uncle Grayson": quoted in Kurlansky, 197.

p. 62: "the opening shot in a war of liberation": ibid., 196.

p. 62: "up against the wall" and "This is a stick-up": ibid.

p. 63: "Stop Columbia's Gym Crow": Columbia University Libraries Online Exhibitions, accessed October 4, 2017, https://exhibitions.cul.columbia.edu/exhibits/show/1968/item/5519.

p. 63: "This is Harlem Heights, not Morningside Heights": quoted in Bradley, 68.

p. 63: What would whites do . . . : ibid.

p. 63: "Did we come here . . . to Low [Library]?" and "IDA MUST GO!": quoted in Obenzinger, 75; quoted in Rudd, 59.

p. 63: "Send Rudd Back to Cuba!" and "Order Is Peace": Obenzinger, 75; Rudd, 58.

p. 63: "Let's head to . . . the gym site!": quoted in Obenzinger, 75.

p. 63: "taking a hostage": quoted in Robert B. Stulberg, "Three Day Rebellion on Campus: A Diary," *Columbia Daily Spectator*, April 26, 1968, 4, http://spectatorarchive.library.columbia.edu/cgi-bin/columbia?a=d&d=cs19680426-01.1.1&e=-------en-20--68162--txt-IN-Columbia----.

p. 65: One protester, for example, shared how he and his black friends . . . : "Columbia in Crisis: A Student Body Revolts," *Columbia Daily Spectator*, December 13, 1999, 16–17, http://spectatorarchive.library.columbia.edu/cgi-bin/columbia?a=d&d=cs19991213-01.2.19&e=-------en-20--1--txt-txIN------.

p. 65: To the black protesters, the SDS members and their followers were indecisive . . . : Bradley, 69.

p. 65: "SDS can stand on . . . the vanguard": ibid.

p. 66: "I'd like to tell you . . . community is taking over": quoted in Jerry L. Avorn, *Up Against the Ivy Wall: A History of the Columbia Crisis* (New York: Atheneum, 1969), 58.

p. 66: "People are hanging out . . . guitars and stuff" and "and we want you to leave": quoted in Halikman, "Self-imposed Segregation," *Columbia Daily Spectator*, April 28, 1993, 8, http://spectatorarchive.library.columbia.edu/cgi-bin/columbia?a=d&d=cs19930428-02.2.12&e=-------en-20--1--txt-txIN------.

p. 66: "Good luck to you . . . still together": quoted in Rudd, 69.

p. 67: "prisoners": quoted in Robert B. Stulberg, "Three Day Rebellion on Campus: A Diary," *Columbia Daily Spectator*, April 26, 1968, 5, http://spectatorarchive.library.columbia.edu/cgi-bin/columbia?a=d&d=cs19680426-01.1.1&e=-------en-20--68162--txt-IN-Columbia----.

p. 69: "a potentially difficult . . . serious injury": quoted in Rudd, 87.

p. 69: "Strike! Strike! Strike!": ibid., 90.

p. 70: "The way to win . . . fight the cops": ibid.

p. 70: But it wasn't until a reunion . . . : ibid., 100.

p. 71: "The worst racism . . . Morningside Heights": quoted in John Kifner, "Columbia's Radicals of 1968 Hold a Bittersweet Reunion," *New York Times,* April 28, 2008, B1.

Robert F. Kennedy by Mark Kurlansky

p. 74: "the machine becomes . . . make it stop": Mario Savio, Sproul Hall Steps, December 2, 1964, Moffitt Library Media Resources Center, University of California, Berkeley, http://www.lib.berkeley.edu/MRC/saviotranscript.html.

People, Get Ready by Susan Campbell Bartoletti

p. 78: "Yip!," "Pee! . . . movement," and "Yippee!": quoted in Hoffman, *Autobiography,* 137.

p. 79: Always had: ibid., 5

p. 79: "let people experience . . . as thoughts" and "get people to act": ibid., 78.

p. 79: "riffing": ibid., 78.

p. 79: didn't trust the media: ibid., 112.

p. 80: "It's so easy . . . an embarrassment": ibid., 105.

p. 80: How else could the Vietnam War . . . : ibid., 129.

p. 80: you had to be there to "see" it: ibid., 136.

p. 80: "act of sado-masochistic folly": "People, Get Ready," YIP flyer, circa January 1968, Federal Bureau of Investigation of New York, File 100-NY-162260: "Youth International Party (Yippies), 1967–1977," posted June 20, 2011, Government Attic website, https://archive.org/stream/Yippies/Yippies%201967-1977_djvu.txt.

p. 80: "Our battle in Chicago . . . the Vietnam War": Hoffman, *Autobiography,* 161.

p. 80: "festival of life": ibid., 142.

p. 80: massive midnight "Yip-in": ibid.; Howard Smith, "Scenes," *Village Voice,* March 21, 1968, reprinted in Tony Ortega, "The Yippies Are Here!! Plans for a Grand Central

Party. Which Will Go Horribly Wrong," *Village Voice*, April 19, 2010, https://www
.villagevoice.com/2010/04/19/the-yippies-are-here-plans-for-a-grand-central-party
-which-will-go-horribly-wrong/; "3,000 Hippies Sing and Hurl Objects in Grand
Central," *New York Times*, March 23, 1968, 33.

p. 81: "berserk," "They began bashing heads without warning," and "merely sharpened
our determination": Hoffman, 142–143. (Hoffman's account differs from the one
given the *New York Times* article cited above, which states that the police charged after
several young people hurled firecrackers.)

p. 81: "shoot to kill" and "shoot to maim": quoted in Kurlansky, 112; "Police Violence:
Shoot to Kill," YouTube, Media Burn Archive, March 6, 2017, accessed July 28, 2017,
https://www.youtube.com/watch?v=O9sKSRrs46Y.

p. 81: "You measure . . . its assimilated conformists": Benny Avni, "An Interview
with Abbie Hoffman," *Tikkun*, July/August 1989, https://www.tikkun.org/nextgen
/julyaugust-1989-full-table-of-contents.

p. 81: "Little did we realize . . . would soon quit": Hoffman, *Autobiography*, 136.

p. 82: "I was the itch . . . to make it happen": ibid., 100.

p. 82: "The long hot summer . . . end of August": "People, Get Ready," YIP flyer,
circa January 1968, Federal Bureau of Investigation of New York, File 100-NY-162260:
"Youth International Party (Yippies), 1967–1977," posted June 20, 2011, Government
Attic website, https://archive.org/stream/Yippies/Yippies%201967-1977_djvu.txt.

p. 82: "battalions of super-potent": Hoffman, *Autobiography*, 145.

p. 83: pouring gasoline: Andy Roberts, "Reservoir Drugs: The Enduring Myth of LSD in the
Water Supply," Psychedelic Press UK, last updated September 15, 2016, http://psypressuk
.com/2014/03/12/reservoir-drugs-the-enduring-myth-of-lsd-in-the-water-supply/.

p. 83: Experts debunked the threat . . . expensive prank: Lisa Krissoff Boehm,
Popular Culture and the Enduring Myth of Chicago, 1871–1968 (New York: Routledge,
2004), 124.

p. 83: three dollars per tab: Edward M. Brecher and the Editors of Consumer Reports,
"How LSD Was Popularized, 1962–1969," chap. 50 in *The Consumers Union Report on
Licit and Illicit Drugs* (Boston: Little, Brown, 1972), Schaffer Library of Drug Policy,
accessed November 4, 2017, http://www.druglibrary.org/schaffer/library/studies/cu/
cu50.html.

p. 83: "There was no end . . . created a myth": Hoffman, *Autobiography*, 145–146.

p. 83: "We never had to pay . . . free coverage": ibid., 146.

p. 84: Rumors and conspiracy theories also serve a function . . . : Michael Martin and Viren Swami, "Why People Believe Conspiracy Theories," *All Things Considered,* NPR, December 11, 2016, http://www.npr.org/2016/12/11/505187974/why-people -believe-conspiracy-theories.

p. 84: "The only thing . . . nothing happens": quoted in "Daley City Under Siege," *Time,* August 30, 1968, 19.

p. 85: "goggles (to protect . . . militant hippies)": "The Compleat Delegate," *Time,* August 30, 1968, 19.

p. 85: "If you're coming . . . armor in your hair": quoted in Ina Jaffe, "1968 Chicago Riot Left Mark on Political Protests," *Weekend Edition Saturday,* NPR, August 23, 2008, http://www.npr.org/templates/story/story.php?storyId=93898277.

p. 85: "As long as I . . . order in Chicago": quoted in "Chicago '68: A Chronology," Chicago '68 website, accessed July 27, 2017, http://chicago68.com/c68chron.html.

p. 86: "Do you want . . . creating a riot": Hoffman, *Autobiography,* 152.

p. 86: "I don't smoke pot. That's a myth": quoted in Kurlansky, 274.

p. 86: "LINCOLN PARK," "chicks who can type (and spell)," and "cats who have wheels," and "Revolution towards a Free Society": original "Yippie!!" undated 8-page flyer, author's personal collection.

p. 86: "terrorists" and "plant bombs": quoted in Hoffman, *Autobiography,* 152.

p. 86: "The welcome mat . . . rolled up" and "secret": ibid., 154.

p. 86: "Pig Power" and "Live High on the Hog": "Chicago Cops Squelch Piggy Nomination," *Montreal Gazette,* August 23, 1968, 2.

p. 87: "If we can't . . . for breakfast": ibid.

p. 87: "Revolution now!" and "The park belongs to the people!": quoted in Kurlansky, 277.

p. 87: "No sleeping in the park": Hoffman, *Autobiography,* 156.

p. 87: "Pigs!" and "Oink-oink!": quoted in Kurlansky, 279.

p. 88: "A newspaper is the lowest thing there is": quoted in Bill Roeder, "Newsmakers," *Newsweek,* May 5, 1975, 55.

p. 89: "See you at eleven o'clock, kid": quoted in Schultz, 103; quoted in Kurlansky, 280.

p. 89: "They dragged me . . . squad car": Hoffman, *Autobiography,* 160.

p. 91: "a game that's just more fun": quoted in Shepard, 36.

p. 91: "One of the worst mistakes . . . become boring": Hoffman, *Autobiography,* 106.

p. 91: "You came up with . . . goddamned silly": quoted in Shepard, 36.

p. 92: "Don't rely on words . . . clues, and vanish": Hoffman, *Revolution,* 29–30.

pp. 92–93: "This is your moment . . . your turn now": Abbie Hoffman, "Reflections on Student Activism: Speech to the First National Student Convention," Rutgers University, February 6, 1988, Anarchist Library, posted October 12, 2011, accessed July 28, 2017, https://theanarchistlibrary.org/library/abbie-hoffman-reflections-on-student -activism.

p. 93: "He didn't die . . . full heart": quoted in Wayne King, "Abbie Hoffman Committed Suicide Using Barbiturates, Autopsy Shows," *New York Times,* April 18, 1989, http://www.nytimes.com/1989/04/19/us/abbie-hoffman-committed-suicide -using-barbiturates-autopsy-shows.html?mcubz=0.

Prague Spring by Mark Kurlansky
p. 95: "generation gap": Kurlansky, 193.

p. 96: "The people were dissatisfied . . . changed the leaders": quoted in Kurlansky, 25; quoted in Declan Kiberd, "At the Core of 1968 Was a Search for Authority Rather Than Subversion," *Irish Times,* May 1, 2008, https://www.irishtimes.com/opinion /at-the-core-of-1968-was-a-search-for-authority-rather-than-subversion-1.919130.

p. 98: "Don't they realize . . . causing me?": quoted in Kurlansky, 240.

p. 100: "For Those Under . . . This Summer": Paul Hofmann, "For Those Under 30, Prague Seems the Right Place to Be This Summer," *New York Times,* August 12, 1968, 13.

p. 100: "The armies of . . . occupying us": quoted in Kurlansky, 292.

p. 101: "I have devoted . . . personal tragedy": Harry Schwartz, *Prague's 200 Days: The Struggle for Democracy in Czechoslovakia* (London: Pall Mall, 1969), 217.

p. 102: "Don't hang . . . succeed tomorrow": quoted in Kurlansky, 305.

p. 102: "It inhibited change": Alexander Dubček, *Hope Dies Last: The Autobiography of Alexander Dubček,* trans. Jiri Hochman (New York: Kodansha, 1993), 165.

p. 102: "I think that in the long run . . . 'aggressive' bloc": quoted in Kurlansky, 287.

Running with Sharp Schticks by David Lubar

p. 104: I looked at *Billboard:* "Billboard 200: Week of January 6, 1968," *Billboard,* accessed July 27, 2017, http://www.billboard.com/charts/billboard-200/1968-01-06.

p. 105: "right out of the window": Flip Wilson, "Riot Suit," track 3 on *Cowboys and Colored People,* Atlantic SD 8149, 1967, vinyl recording.

p. 106: When Dick Gregory talks . . . : "Dick Gregory—Shoveling Snow," YouTube, posted February 18, 2010, https://www.youtube.com/watch?v=aRr5578yHck.

p. 107: "My body is . . . prescription underwear": "Phyllis Diller, 1968, Standup Comedy," YouTube, posted April 8, 2014, 1:45, https://www.youtube.com/watch?v=h6 ljYYQ1YyY.

p. 107: "older than his birthday": Jackie "Moms" Mabley, "Literacy Test," track 16 on *The Best of Moms Mabley,* Mercury SR 61139, 1968, vinyl recording.

p. 108: When Moms Mabley talks about a black man . . . : ibid.

p. 109: "they had to": "Hollywood Palace, February 5, 1966," YouTube, posted September 27, 2013, 8:17, https://www.youtube.com/watch?v=4IoZzYQRZLI.

p. 110: "Lynde and Sues . . . Charles Nelson Reilly": Walter M. Mayes, conversation with the author.

p. 111: "I'm all for school busing . . . in a classroom": Jo Ann Worley, "Cocktail Party," track 2 on disc 2, *The Best of Rowan and Martin's Laugh-In,* Dan Rowan and Dick Martin, Rhino Home Video Retro Vision B00008PHCV, 2003, DVD.

p. 111: "de-escalate" and "That's easy for you to say": ibid.

p. 111: Producer George Schlatter . . . relief valve: "George Schlatter on Comedy and Politics," YouTube, posted July 16, 2013, 1:08, https://www.youtube.com/watch?v=q3 qXKZ1oqwI.

p. 112: "on the only comedy show . . . against the war" and "sit down a month . . . something daring": George Carlin, *Last Words: A Memoir* (New York: Free Press, 2009), 138.

p. 113: "But we are not against . . . something being said": "Pat Paulsen—Freedom to Censor," YouTube, posted March 5, 2011, 0:05, https://www.youtube.com/watch?v=UuJStuIU_DY.

p. 113: "No matter what . . . enormous significance": "Harry Belafonte Interview—Smothers Brothers Comedy Hour," YouTube, posted October 11, 2009, 1:12, https://www.youtube.com/watch?v=1LWcp2b6rfc.

Student Sacrifices by Omar Figueras
p. 123: "lightning meetings": quoted in Poniatowska, 22.

p. 123: "They made us line up . . . breaking piñatas": ibid., 325.

p. 124: "We have been so tolerant . . . allowed to continue": ibid., 45.

p. 125: "Four men dressed . . . out of the building": ibid., 36.

p. 125: "I'm a mother . . . stirring up trouble": ibid., 62.

p. 126: "Who did those kids . . . their semester grades": ibid., 82.

p. 126: "It's the miniskirt that's to blame": ibid.

p. 126: "A child or teenager . . . anger or hysteria": ibid., 83.

p. 127: "'One from the police . . . military'" and "There was a buzz in the crowd": quoted in Richard Nelsson, "How the *Guardian* Reported Mexico City's Tlatelolco Massacre of 1968," *Guardian*, November 11, 2015, https://www.theguardian.com/cities/from-the-archive-blog/2015/nov/12/guardian-mexico-tlatelolco-massacre-1968-john-rodda.

p. 129: "The worst moment . . . I cannot say": ibid.

p. 129: These men—later revealed as the Olimpia Battalion . . . : Poniatowska, 222.

p. 130: Rodda estimated the dead . . . : Richard Nelsson, "How the *Guardian* Reported Mexico City's Tlatelolco Massacre of 1968," *Guardian*, November 11, 2015, https://www.theguardian.com/cities/from-the-archive-blog/2015/nov/12/guardian-mexico-tlatelolco-massacre-1968-john-rodda.

Running into History by Jim Murphy
p. 135: "for those individuals . . . prayer for": quoted in Donovan Vincent, "The Forgotten Story Behind the 'Black Power' Photo from 1968 Olympics," *Toronto Star*, August 7, 2016.

p. 135: "I'll stand with you" and "I thought I would see . . . I saw love": quoted in Rupert Cornwell, "Great Olympic Friendships: John Carlos, Peter Norman and Tommie Smith—Divided by Their Colour, United by the Cause," *Independent,* August 4, 2016, http://www.independent.co.uk/sport/olympics/rio-2016-olympic-friendships-john-carlos-peter-norman-tommie-smith-mexico-city-1968-black-power-7166771.html.

p. 136: "You could have heard . . . eye of a hurricane": quoted in Gary Younge, "The Man Who Raised a Black Power Salute at the 1968 Olympic Games," *Guardian,* March 30, 2012, https://www.theguardian.com/world/2012/mar/30/black-power-salute-1968-olympics. Although attendance estimates vary, we know the stadium was full that day, and a full stadium held 80,000 people.

p. 136: "Go back to Africa!" and "Nazi-like salute": ibid.

p. 136: "the basic principles of the Olympic Games" and "warped mentalities and cracked personalities": quoted in History Channel, "October 17, 1968: Olympic Protesters Stripped of Their Medals," *This Day in History,* History Channel website, http://www.history.com/this-day-in-history/olymic-protesters-stripped-of-their-medals.

p. 136: "They didn't think it out" and "The demonstration . . . I hate it": quoted in Steve Jacobson, "Hines Talking a Great Race These Days," *Los Angeles Times,* June 1, 1991, http://articles.latimes.com/1991-06-01/sports/sp-2321_1_world-record.

p. 137: "Peter was facing . . . suffering alone": quoted in Vincent.

p. 137: "was a moment . . . racial inequality": ibid.

p. 138: "I had a moral obligation . . . [Brundage and the IOC] had": quoted in Gary Younge, "The Man Who Raised a Black Power Salute at the 1968 Olympic Games," *Guardian,* March 30, 2012, https://www.theguardian.com/world/2012/mar/30/black-power-salute-1968-olympics.

p. 139: "I had no idea . . . for all time": ibid.

The Code Wars by Loree Griffin Burns

Rollin Hotchkiss, a prominent biochemist at Rockefeller University during this time period, is said to have quipped of Nirenberg's poly-U experiment and the race it sparked, "The U-2 incident started the cold war, and the U3 incident started the code war." That quote, documented in Peter Lengyel, "Memories of a Senior Scientist: On Passing the Fiftieth Anniversary of the Beginning of Deciphering the Genetic Code," *Annual Review of Microbiology* 66 (2012): 27–38, is the inspiration for the title of this piece.

The original paper documenting Nirenberg's discovery that the genetic code was composed in triplets was published in 1964: Marshall Nirenberg and Philip Leder,

"RNA Codewords and Protein Synthesis. I. The Effect of Trinucleotides upon the Binding of sRNA to Ribosomes," *Science* 145, 1399–1407.

p. 141: "I know that I stand . . . deeply grateful": Marshall Nirenberg, "Marshall W. Nirenberg—Banquet Speech," Nobel Prize website, accessed March 14, 2017, https://www.nobelprize.org/nobel_prizes/medicine/laureates/1968/nirenberg-speech.html.

p. 141: "that the sequence . . . corresponding protein": Francis Crick, *What Mad Pursuit: A Personal View of Scientific Discovery* (New York: Basic Books, 1988), 108.

p. 142: Nirenberg's research history, first job title, and subsequent research plans: Portugal, chapter 6.

p. 142: "as an independent investigator . . . the deck running": Marshall Nirenberg, "Historical Review: Deciphering the Genetic Code—A Personal Account," *Trends in Biochemical Sciences* 29 (2004): 47.

p. 142: "It is suicidal": ibid.

p. 143: Nirenberg's rejection from the 1961 Colds Spring Harbor Symposium: Robert G. Martin, "A Revisionist View of the Breaking of the Genetic Code," chapter 14 in *NIH: An Account of Research in Its Laboratories and Clinics,* ed. DeWitt Stetten Jr. (Orlando, FL: Academic Press, 1984), 285.

p. 143: Anecdotes about the RNA Tie Club: James D. Watson, *Genes, Girls, and Gamow* (New York: Knopf, 2002); Portugal, chapters 4 and 5; James D. Watson, *The Annotated and Illustrated Double Helix* (New York: Simon & Schuster, 2012), 132, 245, and 248.

p. 144: The formula Crick came up with for the flow of genetic information in cells, DNA → RNA → Protein, is commonly referred to as "the central dogma" of molecular biology. It remains so, although amendments have been made to accommodate new understandings.

p. 144: Nirenberg's thoughts on his code-breaking experiments: Dr. Ruth Roy Harris, interviews with Marshall Nirenberg, September 20, 1995, to January 24, 1996, NIH History website, https://history.nih.gov/archives/downloads/Nirenberg%20oral%20history%20Chap%205-%20%20Nobel%20Prize.pdf.

p. 145: Nirenberg and Matthaei's poly-U experiments: Marshall W. Nirenberg, J. Heinrich Matthae, and Oliver W. Jones, "An Intermediate in the Biosynthesis of Polyphenylalanine Directed by Synthetic Template RNA," *Proceedings of the National Academy of Sciences* 48 (1962): 104–109, https://www.ncbi.nlm.nih.gov/pmc/articles/PMC285511/?page=1.

p. 145: Nirenberg's appearance at the Fifth International Congress of Biochemistry in Moscow in 1961 is described in many of the works already mentioned, and its importance in science history is highlighted in E. C. Slater, "54 Years of International Congresses of Biochemistry and Molecular Biology," *IUBMB Life* 55, no. 4–5 (May 2003): 185–187.

p. 146: Severo Ochoa's reaction to Nirenberg's Moscow bombshell: Peter Lengyel, "Memories of a Senior Scientist: On Passing the Fiftieth Anniversary of the Beginning of Deciphering the Genetic Code," *Annual Review of Microbiology* 66 (2012): 27–38.

p. 147: "I thought that was . . . take a vacation": quoted in Portugal, 91.

p. 147: James Watson's reading of a newspaper during the presentation: Dr. Ruth Roy Harris, interviews with Marshall Nirenberg, September 20, 1995, to January 24, 1996, NIH History website, https://history.nih.gov/archives/downloads/Nirenberg%20oral %20history%20Chap%205-%20%20Nobel%20Prize.pdf. His habit of tuning out speakers that bored him by reading was noted by many others and is described, for example, in Robert Olby, *The Path to the Double Helix* (Seattle: University of Washington Press, 1974), 298.

p. 148: "We at NIH were . . . and Heinrich's discovery": Robert G. Martin, "A Revisionist View of the Breaking of the Genetic Code," chapter 14 in *NIH: An Account of Research in Its Laboratories and Clinics* (Orlando, FL: Academic Press, 1984), 294.

p. 148: "I tried my best . . . a few months": ibid., 293.

p. 150: "magic circle": quoted in Portugal, 47.

Douglas Engelbart by Marc Aronson
p. 156: To see Engelbart's actual demonstration, visit Stanford University's MouseSite Digital Archive: http://web.stanford.edu/dept/SUL/library/extra4/sloan/mousesite /1968Demo.html.

SELECTED BIBLIOGRAPHY

Bradley, Stefan M. *Harlem vs. Columbia University: Black Student Power in the Late 1960s.* Chicago: University of Illinois Press, 2009.

Hoffman, Abbie. *The Autobiography of Abbie Hoffman.* New York: Four Walls Eight Windows, 1980.

———. *Revolution for the Hell of It.* New York: Thunder's Mouth Press, 1968.

Kurlansky, Mark. *1968: The Year That Rocked the World.* New York: Random House, 2004.

Lao Tzu. *Tao Te Ching.* Translated by Jonathan Star. New York: Jeremy P. Tarcher/Putnam, 2001.

Obenzinger, Hilton. *Busy Dying.* Victoria, TX: Chax, 2008.

Poniatowska, Elena. *Massacre in Mexico.* Translated by Helen R. Lane. New York: Viking, 1975.

Portugal, Franklin. *The Least Likely Man: Marshall Nirenberg and the Discovery of the Genetic Code.* Cambridge: MIT Press, 2015.

Rudd, Mark. *Underground: My Life with SDS and the Weathermen.* New York: Morrow, 2009.

Schultz, Jon. *No One Was Killed: The Democratic National Convention.* Chicago: University of Chicago Press, 2009.

Shen, Fan. *Gang of One.* Lincoln: University of Nebraska Press, 2004.

Shepard, Benjamin. *Play, Creativity, and Social Movements: If I Can't Dance, It's Not My Revolution.* London: Routledge, 2011.

Stern, Michael. "Walkout Disrupts Memorial to King." *Columbia Daily Spectator,* April 10, 1968, 1–3. http://spectatorarchive.library.columbia.edu/cgi-bin/columbia?a=d&d=cs19680410-01.1.1&e=-------en-20--1--txt-txIN------.

Tye, Larry. *Bobby Kennedy: The Making of a Liberal Icon.* New York: Random House, 2017.

IMAGE CREDITS

INDEX